Praise for

Half a Life

"Truly exceptional . . . elegant, painful, stunningly honest . . . [We watch] a writer of fine fiction . . . probe, directly, carefully and with great humility, the source from which his fiction springs. . . . huge and . . . heartbreaking."
—DANI SHAPIRO, *The New York Times Book Review*

"A lyrical and haunting memoir . . . a simple yet remarkable story about pain and guilt, maturity and responsibility, hope and understanding." —*San Francisco Chronicle*

"I recently went on a trip with a couple of friends, one of whom brought along *Half a Life*. The book's slender enough that the three of us devoured it in three days—and beautifully written enough that we spent the rest of the trip discussing it. . . . Too many memoirs suffer from lack of perspective. But Strauss explores memory, guilt, and coming-of-age from a mature vantage point that leads to enormous insight. . . . You may have heard Strauss tell this tale on NPR's *This American Life*. Here's the written version, by a terrific storyteller who doesn't waste a word. [Grade:] **A**." —*Entertainment Weekly*

"Strauss is a heralded novelist [and *Half a Life*] is painfully raw and beautifully written." —*Los Angeles Times*

"Darin Strauss has spent a good part of his adult life reliving, regretting and reflecting on a single, split-second incident. . . . *Half a Life* is a starkly honest account of that fateful moment and his life thereafter. . . . Strauss doesn't just stick to anecdotes that highlight his genuine empathy and deeply held guilt; he is gutsy [and] candid. . . . Strauss's story is a penetrating, thought-provoking examination of the human mind."

— *The Washington Post*

"[*Half a Life*] inspires admiration, sentence by sentence. . . . This artfully and simply presented book could be read in a few hours, but its intensity commands more attention. This is a memoir in its finest form, a fully imagined and bittersweet book that transcends a single misstep."

—*Chicago Tribune* (Editor's Choice)

"Subtle, exceptional . . . It is a rare privilege to make the trip of *Half a Life*. What might have been exploitative instead feels important, and dearly won."   —*The Plain Dealer*

"With honesty and sensitivity, Strauss looks not only at how that fateful incident decades ago ended [a] young life but also at how it greatly affected his . . . lyrical and haunting."

—*San Francisco Chronicle*

"Spare, wrenching, and painfully generous . . . riveting [and] sad . . . brilliant."   —*New York*

"*Half a Life,* a remarkable, beyond-brave memoir . . . offers an intensely personal look at the most agonizing events. . . . Nothing goes excused or unexamined. With astounding frequency, Strauss pinpoints truths that most of us would find indescribable, and ultimately arrives at an insight as profound as it is impossible to accept."   —*O: The Oprah Magazine*

"*Half a Life* is an unusually honest, thoughtful, and unsettling memoir, which readers and critics are destined to call 'brave'— for it is brave. But the book is more than simply brave; it is a searingly self-disciplined work of literature, and of self-examination. Darin Strauss does not permit himself even one sentence, even one moment, of lazy thinking or mitigating excuses. He examines with rigorous honesty every moment of the most awful and tragic event of his life. After all that admirable work and all that attentive detail, when he does finally reach a place of cautious hope, the impact is staggering and unforgettable."

—ELIZABETH GILBERT, author of *Eat, Pray, Love*

"Darin Strauss's *Half a Life* is the best anything I've read—novel, memoir, story—in a very long time. Incredibly, it's also the most moving. (And inspiring, and challenging; it's a book that asks you to live up to it.) This book has the greatest weight-to-power ratio I've ever seen. Read it, be swallowed, come out changed. If you've faced a death, of course you should read it. But everyone faces a life, and so the rest of us should read it too."

—DAVID LIPSKY, author of *Absolutely American*

"A story of hope and what it means to be human."

—CARRIE FISHER, author of *Wishful Drinking*

"This book will break your heart. It's about the big and important things that happen before you are ready for them and how they shape your life. It's a tragedy and a coming-of-age story. Mostly, it's a great and moving book about a boy becoming a man, and it belongs on the shelf with just a precious few others—*The Catcher in the Rye, The Moviegoer, Joe Gould's Secret*. It should be read and reread. It's a treasure."

—RICH COHEN, author of *Tough Jews* and *Sweet and Low*

"I've read so many memoirs. Darin Strauss's is more honest and useful than all of them rolled together, including my own. This might be the bravest book you will ever read."

—KELLY CORRIGAN, author of *The Middle Place* and *Lift*

Also by Darin Strauss

Chang and Eng
The Real McCoy
More Than It Hurts You

HALF A LIFE

HALF A LIFE

A Memoir

Darin Strauss

Random House Trade Paperbacks
New York

2011 Random House Trade Paperback Edition

Copyright © 2010 by Darin Strauss
Reading group guide copyright © 2011 by Random House, Inc.

Published in the United States by
Random House Trade Paperbacks,
an imprint of The Random House Publishing Group,
a division of Random House, Inc., New York.

RANDOM HOUSE TRADE PAPERBACKS and colophon
are trademarks of Random House, Inc.
RANDOM HOUSE READER'S CIRCLE and colophon
is a trademark of Random House, Inc.

Originally published in hardcover in the United States by McSweeney's in 2010.

Library of Congress Cataloging-in-Publication Data
Strauss, Darin.
Half a life : a memoir / Darin Strauss. — 2011 Random House Trade Paperback ed.
p. cm.
"Originally published in hardcover in the United States by McSweeney's in
2010"—T.p. verso.
ISBN 978-0-8129-8253-4
eBook ISBN 978-0-679-64382-1
1. Strauss, Darin. 2. Authors, American—21st century—Biography. 3. Life change
events. I. Title.
PS3569.T692245Z47 2011
813'.54—dc22
[B]
2010052484

Printed in the United States of America

www.randomhousereaderscircle.com

246897531

For my parents, and hers.

1

"By the time you've run your mind through it a hundred times, relentlessly worked out every tic of your terror, it's lost its power over you . . . [Soon it's] a story on a page, or, more precisely, everybody's story on a page."

—John Gardner

Half my life ago, I killed a girl.

I had just turned eighteen, and when you drive in new post-adolescence, you drive with friends. We were headed to shoot a few rounds of putt-putt. It was May 1988. The breeze did its open-window work on the hair behind my neck and ears. We had a month before high-school gradua-tion. I was at the wheel. Up ahead, on the right shoulder, a pair of tiny bicyclists bent over their handlebars. The hori-zon was just my town's modest skyline done in watercolors. We all shared a four-lane road; the bicycles traveled in the same direction as my car. Bare legs pedaling under a long sky. I think I fiddled with the radio. Hey what song is this? So turn it up. Then one of the bike riders did something. I remember only that—a glitch on the right. My Oldsmo-bile stayed in the far left lane. After a wobble or two, the bicyclist eased a wheel into the road, maybe thirty feet away. My tires lapped up the distance that separated us.

Next the bicycle made a crisp turn into the left lane and my sudden car. Dark blond hair appeared very clearly in my windshield. I remember a kind of mechanical curiosity about why this was happening and what it might mean.

This moment has been, for all my life, a kind of shadowy giant. I'm able, tick by tick, to remember each second before it. Radio; friends; thoughts of mini-golf, another thought of maybe just going to the beach; the distance between car and bicycle closing: anything could still happen. But I am powerless to see what comes next; the moment raises a shoulder, lowers its head, and slumps away.

And then it's too late. My forearm hooks to protect my eyes. The front-seat passenger shouts. I picture my foot disappearing under the dash, kicking down for the brake, straining farther than any real leg can go. Yet the hood of my Oldsmobile met Celine Zilke at forty miles an hour. Her head cracked the windshield. I remember the yellow reflector from her spokes, a useless spark, kicking up the glass incline and over the roof.

My car bumped onto the grassy median. And then I must have done all the normal driver things. Put on the clonking hazards, rolled to a stop, cut the engine; I must have stepped onto the grass in my T-shirt and shorts. I simply have no memory of how I got there.

Celine Zilke, the girl on I killed, was sixteen and always will be sixteen. And I knew her: Celine went to my school. She was an eleventh-grader. I see her playing field hockey in blue gym shorts—Celine had been that lively, athletic type one always imagines in shorts. Or I see her settled in beside friends on the concrete benches just outside the cafeteria, or dashing off notes in the public-speaking class we took together. Celine sat by the window.

When I look back now, she strikes me most of all as young.

I walked to where Celine lay on the road. I didn't know who I'd hit or even that we'd had a serious collision. I thought in terms of broken arms and getting in trouble with my parents. Then I reached her and noticed the peculiar stillness of her face. This stillness transformed her—I didn't even recognize her. The eyes were open, but her gaze seemed to extend only an inch or so. This openness that does not project out is the image I have of death: everything present, nothing there. She lay on the warm macadam in oblique angles—arm bent up and out, foot settled under a knee. In the skin between her eyebrows there was a small, imprinted purple horseshoe of blood.

"I think maybe she's hurt," said my friend Dave. We couldn't tell if there was any life coming from her pale, parted mouth. *Maybe she's hurt* might pass for an obvious statement when you read it now, but it didn't as we stood over Celine on that morning. Her face looked relaxed, as if she were lost in thought. Yet I could feel my own breathing speed up. And that's all I felt.

A tragedy's first act is crowded with supporting players: witnesses crimping their faces, policemen scribbling in pads and making radio calls, EMS guys unfolding equipment, tubes and wheels.

I must have managed to ask how Celine was doing, because at some point a policeman told me that she was unconscious but holding on. I remember talk of cardiac arrest, of a medevac helicopter coming to take her to the hospital. I had a somewhat thickheaded sensation that everyone was responding appropriately to what was clearly a crisis. But I still didn't think there was any reason to freak out. This was something fixable; it was *being* fixed. Still, I had been careful not to stand anyplace where I could see Celine again—her face's semblance of musing calm, her unnatural position.

Police had suspended traffic on the highway's two sides. My friends made cameo appearances as standers, mullers, back rubbers. I thought how strange it was that, in normal life, we all touched so rarely. Traffic, I now understood—I'd started to think abstractly—is a kind of stream crowded with fish, a rush of momentum, and we'd been yanked to the side of the brook and forced to dry in the sun. I'd become one of those sights I'd driven past a hundred times on the expressway, the locus of a thousand strangers' curiosity.

That's the thing about shock. You can have these clear and selfish perceptions, as you circle without looking at the truth lying alone on the street.

The most embarrassing memory of that day came when two teenage girls materialized from one of the stopped cars nearby. I heard the thunk of doors closing. And next the young women came walking over the grass. They were sexy and not from my school. Both wore shorts and white sleeveless undershirts; one smelled, optimistically, of suntan oil.

"Hey," she said. "You in that crash?"—her voice a mix of apprehension and prying.

"Yeah," I said.

"Wow—oh, man."

"I know."

"You all right?"

"Yeah," I said, "I am, thanks," and walked away.

Having acknowledged my own centrality and drama, and sensing the girls were still watching, I dropped to my knees and covered my head with my hands—fingers between the ears and temples, like a man who's just won the US Open. This plagiarized "emotional" reaction, acted out for girls I'd never see again, is one more stomach-turning fact of that afternoon.

"Aww," the girls said, coming over to me. "You know it wasn't your fault."

I didn't even nod—I just got up and showboated away from them, shoulders back; I went over to the bustle around Celine, the bustle from which these girls were excluded. I can only explain it like this: there was still a disconnect between me and the realness of what was happening.

I've come to see our central nervous system as a kind of vintage switchboard, all thick foam wires and old-fashioned plugs. The circuitry isn't properly equipped; after a surplus of emotional information the system overloads, the circuit breaks, the board runs dark. That's what shock is.

My father arrived. Someone must have called him, though this was before cell phones. It was the sight of my dad that day, the clean sadness on his face, that turned this real, finally. All this had happened to me; I had done this; I was his son. Dad was somehow like a new circuit in the fuse box. He arrived, emotion could flow. In his hug I went out all at once into tears, as I never had before and haven't since.

I don't remember how long we'd all been there, whether I'd gone to look at Celine's excessively pale face again. (A psychologist later told me such memory skips have been installed for our own protection. Trauma makes a spark that in a white glow washes out details, guilt, shame—a flare that throws the recent past into shadow and deep obscurity.)

A policeman shambled over. His eyes glided across my face; he asked me clipped questions. How fast had I been going? Had I been drinking? (*About forty, I guess,* and *No, no. Jesus, no.*) Someone, perhaps a new EMS arrival, finally took charge. All right, folks—step *back.* He decided on the best way to transport Celine. The how of his plan escaped me, and still does. But an ambulance did wheel in and get Celine, finally and somehow, away from all the stopped cars. They took her to the hospital. And my passengers Mike and Jeff—twin friends who'd been in the backseat—also managed to get out of there. And then, after the traffic was unjammed; after the police told me I was "free to go"; and with a suddenness and ease out of sync with the scale of what was happening—it seemed a form of insanity to touch the car again—my dad just slipped into the driver's seat. Dave took Dad's car, I fell into mine beside my father, and we were off. I sat in the front passenger seat. A crack in the car's windshield measured the length of the glass. Sunlight caught in tendrils that raked out from its sides.

My parents, after offering the quiet-voiced inevitables, told me not to beat myself up about it.

I don't remember what Dave and I did the rest of that afternoon. I certainly didn't phone Celine's family. She and I hadn't known each other—not well enough, or really much at all—and so I was too afraid to phone, or even to look up the Zilkes in the white pages.

"You should go to a movie," my parents told me, trying their best.

A benign suggestion, maybe, but I didn't want to be *seen* trying to enjoy myself. Judging by the EMS workers' concerned brows, I was afraid Celine might actually die. She could already be dead. I didn't want to appear capable of any emotion but remorse—so I traveled to a theater in some other town. I must have believed that keeping up a picture of constant remorse was the same, morally, as living in constant remorse. That night, Dave and I drove down near the county line to see *Stand and Deliver*.

Heading to the multiplex, the weirdness of being out, of not being under house arrest, settled on me like ash. (Shouldn't I have at least considered visiting Celine's hospital room?)

Before *Stand and Deliver* had even started, in the lobby I came across a guy from my town. (Why visit her hospital room, though? What could I offer?)

In one of those coincidences that life hands over more realistically than fiction can, the guy in the lobby was my good friend, Jim.

Jim jogged up to me on line at the ticket booth. "Heard what happened," he said.

"Yeah," I said. "I didn't see her until it was too late," I apologized.

"Holy shit," he said. Was there something *off* about his facial presentation? Where was the concern, or even a little solemnity? I sensed something weird in him right away—mockery nibbling there at the side of his mouth—and now he raised his hands, palms out. Next, a high-pitched "Ahhh!" Then: "Please! Don't run me down!" And then more comic squeals, little darts tossed in the air.

Dave showed Jim an eloquent frown, quit it, quit it.

But next, an even nastier sound: Jim's slashing laugh. He was cracking up at me.

Dave's appalled stare, the shuffling feet of a conversation breaking down. Then Jim said, "No, you're upset? Really? Come on, hey. Nothing wrong with a joke. What's wrong with a joke?"

Everything. I felt panicky and bright and swollen: hugely sad, acutely *seen.* I slouched away, tucked myself into the theater's dark, and had a sense of being extinguished.

The letup in perception, the no-input cluelessness—that's the kind of shock everyone's familiar with. But shock is not a one-time event. That system-junking you experience at the start goes away, of course. But then a lesser shock keeps showing up, to hurl a big muffling blanket over you. And when you push out of *that,* you feel it almost as a sudden blinking exposure to light. I'm talking about how your mind behaves after the broken circuit *appears* to be back up and running. I mean, why did I feel half-okay there in the multiplex parking lot, and why had I continued to feel that way until Jim's cackle? The truth about shock, and about our bodies, is that they don't want us to feel things deeply. We're designed to act, react, forget; to be shallow. I knew I was normal—I had been a normal, normally embraced person twenty-four hours before. But would a normal person feel even halfway okay, as I seemed to feel now? Was it as if I'd somehow *forgotten* the accident?

Well, I remembered, of course. I remembered without end. In fact, one *me* kept remembering how another *me* from a second ago had just remembered the maybe life-destroying horror on West Shore Road (destroying, perhaps, two lives). And I'd remember how I'd just been enduring *that* a second ago—and catch myself remembering it. And *then* I'd remember her reflector scuttling up the windshield, the sensation of my working to swerve, the surprise of her being so close and detailed. It wasn't really *me* feeling it at any one time—rather, I was remembering those other *me*s, and we each shared it together, and all of us were overly compassionate to one another.

And here's a cruel truth: the more accurate thing is that I kept *sort of* remembering without end. My brain persisted—as any bodily organ would—in trying to heal what was in effect a bruise. The bruise was the memory. And to remain what I thought of as human, I had to keep fighting against my basic, animal, healing response. That's what the first day was like. The sensation I was fighting is maybe close to denial. But it's not exactly denial.

My fear now is that all of this sounds over-aestheticized, and vague. There were times when the size of what had happened felt like a kind of nauseated grin: I'd done something this incalculably big, and here I was, still alive. I was okay. I'd hit a girl with my car, but the way the world worked I wasn't in jail, I wasn't hurt; I was free to indulge in a movie. It was this thought that made me leave the movie before it ended. The part of the brain that isn't automatic is an imagining machine, feeling all possibilities of feeling: it keeps pushing its way into this marshy, pleasant terrain. You struggle against that push, and start to feel your stomach protest. It's not so much even a type of consciousness as it is a circumstance, into which you pass by slow degrees. I've never seen this sufficiently examined. It mutates into a less-unreal reality that still seems different, somehow, than being fully present. Self-hate is rarely un-conditional. I don't pretend it's all right that I felt even half-okay.

At home in bed that first night I had patchy, mundane dreams about normal things.

It would be nobler and less uncomfortable to write that I tossed sleeplessly. Or that I woke with a scooped-out pain in my gut. Or that I sat down in my underwear at my desk that had moonlight on it and I had the terrible sense one gets, after something irrevocable, of being in the wrong place—of having awakened into a new and cramped world. (This is the sense I would have, on many nights, later.) I ended up scouring through details of the day: those EMS guys talking about cardiac arrest, about loss of blood, about not liking her chances. I homed in on that word—"chances," with its promise of upside—and not on how the paramedic's voice had tightened, the odds seizing his throat.

So few of our days contain actions that are irrevocable. Our lives are *designed* not to allow for anything irrevocable. The school part of our lives continues to be the school part for eighteen years, the work parts stay the work parts, and if we're lucky nothing disarranges them; the small inconsistencies get buried under talk, explanations, rescheduling. If everything couldn't continue as planned, no real plans could be made. But the breakfasts and TV afternoons and band practices of teenaged life had been disrupted by something irrevocable, and I was new to it. And how did I handle this? What I want to write is that I lay there until morning, with tear-stained eyes, a tear-stained pillow, a tear-stained life. What can one do with levels of gloom and guilt, fear and disbelief, of bewilderment above one's capacity to register?

I slept soundly.

A police officer called the next morning to say that Celine had died in the hospital. It was unclear whether her parents, who had been on vacation, had been able to see her.

My father answered the phone. The officer never asked for me.

My surest memories of that day are the reflector running up the windshield and the sunshine in the cracks as Dad got me home. I can *imagine* the flash of impact, of course. Even if I'm unable to really call back much about it. But it's not hard to guess at the terrible, scratched-out details.

The truth is, anyone with a TV can fill this scene, taking snippets from the editing floor, plug-ins from the visual and sound-effects library we all carry. Pretty girl on bike, a shy little thud, hysterical windshield. And I'm somewhere in there too, trying to swerve, trying to disappear.

The police, Celine's biking companion, and the recollection of five cars' worth of eyewitnesses all conspired to declare me blameless. No charges were filed. A police detective named Paul Vitucci later told the newspaper, "For an unknown reason, her bicycle swerved into what you might call the traffic portion of the street, and she was immediately struck by the car. There was no way he"—meaning me—"could have avoided the accident, no way whatsoever."

I remember coming down to breakfast, and my parents showing me that article. I remember thinking two things. 1) I am fine. The sweet, marshy part felt—*You made it*. And the other part said 2) Well, that's it, I'm in the paper for the world to read about, there is no hiding from this. And I was right. After the story appeared in the local paper, everyone did find out. One friend of mine who lived about an hour north was startled awake by his mother with the news.

I'm sure my parents worried about me, but I don't remember what they said, and I don't think they tried to make contact with Celine's family.

Very soon I got to the article's denouement: Vitucci, eyewitnesses, unprovisional absolution. Society was clearing me. But how could any reporter be so certain? If I hadn't been with my friends, felt them next to me and in the backseat—if I hadn't tried to point all of us toward something fun—maybe I would have focused on Celine, or driven slower. Or honked sooner. (Though I was positive that I had honked, when I'd first seen her inch away from the shoulder and into the right lane.) Any of ten different actions on my part might have led to an alternate ending. Maybe I hadn't felt the right amount of alarm, just before the girl jumped across two lanes.

On a map Long Island looks like a tailless crocodile with its mouth open. Its far shore yawns into a pair of peninsulas a hundred miles east of New York City, and the crocodile's hind-end nestles right up against Manhattan. Not too far up the crocodile's back sits Glen Head, my town: the patch of low, paved swampland where Celine and I went to school, at North Shore High.

Manhattan casts a thin shadow onto Long Island. For most people, life in Glen Head verged on total disconnection from the city—ours could have been any suburb, anywhere—though when traffic was easy it took us just a half hour to reach tall and shaded Midtown.

As you drive the Long Island Expressway toward North Shore High School, the city relaxes its grip on the land. Soon you're in the middle of wide suburban ho-humness. Though western Long Island differs from a real country milieu in all kinds of major ways (traffic snags, no silos), it's true that North Shore High—only a public school despite the upscale name, largely middle-class Italian and middle-class Irish—was small enough for everyone to know everyone else's business.

Which meant many uncomfortable things. This wasn't

close to first among my worries and sadnesses, but it would be a lie to pretend it wasn't somewhere in my thoughts: I'd violated the primary rule of junior and senior high—*don't get people talking about you too much*. This was wearing the brightest shirt on the playground. This was Mom giving you a kiss in the lobby. The thought of returning to school made me feel swollen and incandescent again. I was disgraced, I was blessed (alive and journalistically absolved). I would be cafeteria news, the object of a discreetly pointed finger or nod. I would be the heavy dark ingot from the adult world—the world of consequences—introduced into the nothing-counts ethos of adolescence.

So here's the next stage of guilt: when it's about to become social. There were two parts of me that I wanted to keep above water: a respect for Celine, and a concern for her family. That seemed right and maybe even selfless. But the water that kept lapping over was this: how would people see me? *How do I keep the accident from being the main thing about me forever?*

Immature, offensive thoughts—someone died.

I stayed away from school for almost a week. (I'd already gotten into college, and so was pretty sure I was risking absolutely nothing by skipping all those classes.) The days after the movie-theater mistake and the announcement of Celine's death I spent behind my bedroom door, talking to no one in particular. I was more parrot than person—a parrot in underpants and socks, repeating his one cry. "How seriously will *I* be messed up by this?"

Which is *itself,* I don't have to tell you, a pubescently egocentric thing to wonder. My concern about Celine, in those first days, was in large part really for that future version of myself—that he not become a shadowy and impaired figure. A week before I'd been eighteen and getting ready to push off for college, for love (I'd imagined) plus adventures with friends, then some cool and genial job. When my brain focused on losing all that, I became twitchy and frightened and horrible. At the same time, this anxiety triggered a new guilt: I should not be thinking about something so self-centered. I would concentrate on Celine's parents, and next (after the shiver passing through who I was; after the cold squeeze in the throat) on nothing. The muffling blanket would fall over my thoughts. I'd hear something distinctly: the hinge sound of a book I opened, or my own breath.

One morning—Monday?—I left my room and went downstairs. A silent planet. Parents away at work, younger sister at school. I walked through the numbed rooms, stopping to read—because I was still allowed to take pleasure in magazines, right?—a *Sports Illustrated.* (Companies kept printing them, which meant time was still trudging ahead.) A photo of Danny Manning driving to the basket. How to face down a Nolan Ryan fastball. Can anyone fill John "The Wizard of Westwood" Wooden's shoes? I've already read this stupid issue. And it was this second thought that cleared everything out. I was the kid I'd been three days ago. The morning passed with the sluggish, dusty feeling that comes to people when they're loafing. But then, at the fridge, I was stopped by what struck me as a presentiment. Maybe I'd be okay right now if I could only get myself to remember—what? To remember or realize *what*? And I stood in the kitchen with a glass in my hand and tried to figure out what that what was.

"We need to have you over at the accident site in a car," said the Shrink. "What say you?"

He was middle-aged, a gray and not very fit fifty—thrown together, it seemed, from sausage meat and behaviorism classes.

"No, seriously," he said, "that's what you need today, is to drive that road again."

"Um," I said. How could I just pop over to where I'd killed Celine? (This was, I think, four days after that nightmare morning. It also happened to be my first therapy session ever.) "Okay," I said. I was blushing to the edge of tears. "Sure, I guess."

The Shrink—"Let's do it!"—smacked the arms of his chair. And he sought, with quick vanity, the reflection in a big mirror opposite him. Just as fast he turned away. He appeared to have reached that situation of health where vanity meant you *didn't* risk your face in the mirror.

"Hey, come on now, Darin—you only *guess?* How about if I told you we're going to go in my Porsche?"

I swear this is what he said.

West Shore Road follows the turns of the Long Island Sound like a tag-along sister. This Tuesday a.m. it had the dispiriting vibe of all empty beachfronts in the rain.

Canadian geese bummed around the median where my own car, pretty much a few moments before, had slid to its stop. Where I'd stood and performed for those girls with their what-have-we-here faces.

"Let me show you," the Shrink was saying about his Porsche, "what this baby can do zero-to-sixty, in *awesome* time." (This really was his method, but I'm not sure what it says about the profession—whether this is psychotherapy or just Long Island psychotherapy, where all problems can be extenuated by making good time on the L.I.E.)

He stepped hard on the gas. The rain kept on as gentle drizzle, making an occasional plonk against the windshield. The Shrink ignored the street to focus his somewhat buggy eyes on me. He'd studied Judd Hirsch in *Ordinary People,* and was trying to be the hearty Jewish man to rescue me. West Shore Road offers two lanes in each direction. Maybe my *Ordinary People* foreboding was just that I'd seen the movie, and so was on guard for any resonances. In any case, it felt less like my moment than a pop culture remake I wanted to avoid. The drops on his windshield—the Porsche really was aerodynamic—had reversed field; they were traveling *up,* shivering in little broken dashes. But the Shrink didn't flick on his wipers. He futzed with the tape player, still eyeing me. His hair had Bozo-grade kinks at the temples. Let's just say he failed to come off doctorially. His car, I couldn't help noticing—I am Long Island born and bred—wasn't the splashy 911 model that the frequent automotive name-dropping had led me to expect. Rather, it was a 944, what I knew to be the "Starter Porsche." This model used Volkswagen parts. My hands were stuck in my jeans pockets, up to my thin sweaty wrists. Here I was, nipping along with a man who meant to save me in a souped-up Beetle. Cockeyed is maybe more accurate than buggy-eyed. But any man who tries to push into an emotional conversation—and to lead it to a very specific payoff—while entertaining the pleasures of driving really fast and dreamily on a wet road will of necessity seem bug-eyed. His stereo played "Let's Hear It for the Boy," from the *Footloose* soundtrack. It was obvious the Shrink felt a large and human pride in his purring German go-getter. He pronounced the brand properly, with the vocal pirouette of a *sha* at the end.

He decelerated—"Here?" he said. "Is this where?"—and even I noticed how smartly the eager little machine gunned down to lawful speeds.

I followed the pointer of his finger. "Um," I said. "Not sure."

If I'd tried to go beyond those short words, my voice would have guttered. I had already shared too much of what I felt and knew; I longed to feel and know *more*. "Maybe?" I said.

The sky had dropped a curtain on the sun. I remember the fast-passing median and its luscious grass. I can still see the boring road. The Shrink slowed us even more. Some geese poked along the median, each in its own way. I went nauseous. The day had become grim, irreparable.

"Okay, so?" he said, a wink of the profession in his voice. "How do you feel?"

What could I possibly have offered as an answer?

Then the sky bailed me out.

"Hey, look at *that*," said the Shrink. A long leg of sunlight kicked down through the fog.

Miraculously, I could perform all the rites of conversation again.

"I feel pretty good?" Somehow I didn't let the tears fall. "Not bad?" My voice wasn't even really a sniveling whisper.

So I tried to give this a chance. I tried—after the Porsche edged onto the shoulder, stopping next to a sweep of West Shore Road. The *Footloose* soundtrack had forged ahead: first to "Almost Paradise (Love Theme from *Footloose*)," now Bonnie Tyler's "Holding Out for a Hero." After a moment of tiptoeing around the mood, the Shrink twisted the volume all the way down. We sat together in soft ticking silence. I tried to chuck my guilt into the landscape's calm. I tried. And it *was* weird to be back here. Only days later, and it was already just a spot. A spot with geese and a spear of light.

Your muscles can tense with hope. I looked around for somewhere I could entrust with all this emotion: the khaki stripe of sand a little way off; the clean bend of street that (in a guess) I'd picked as the exact place where the accident had happened; all the vast and true stuff that seems to be nearly revealed, but isn't, when you take the time to admire nature—that is in fact never revealed.

But a sickly paste of anxiety covered everything. I feared

that by giving my feeling over to someone *else's* idea of what I should be feeling, I'd lose it. Years later, at college, I would read a Hemingway story about a young man home from a war, and the words would be so right I'd see that Porsche and that median strip and my stomach would turn heavy:

> Krebs found that to be listened to at all he had to lie, and after he had done this twice he, too, had a reaction against the war and against talking about it . . .
>
> His lies were quite unimportant lies and consisted in attributing to himself things other men had seen, done or heard of . . .
>
> Krebs acquired the nausea in regard to experience that is the result of untruth or exaggeration, and when he occasionally met another man who had really been a soldier and they talked a few minutes in the dressing room at a dance he fell into the easy pose of the old soldier among other soldiers: that he had been badly, sickeningly frightened all the time.
>
> In this way he lost everything.

Over the Shrink's Porsche clouds were tapping together, and the sky turned dismal again. The occasional car passed to slide its lights over the road. I had a fresh, healthy thought: It was too soon for me to gain anything meaningful from being here.

The Shrink turned a key, and his car snorted awake. "This," he said, "was a help, right—this drive?"

I lied and I nodded: It sure had been.

His pink face (which for all I know wasn't nearly as vulgar as I still need to see it) eased into the smile he'd wanted to wear all along. And the Porsche skimmed back onto what you might call the traffic portion of the street.

"I *knew* it, Darin. It's just a place. The accident's just something that happened. This happened to both of you."

Still, the Shrink needed to get back at me for having doubted him. He did this, however, with the gentlest touch. "Listen, you probably don't understand this yet, but therapy," he said, "is a process, okay?" He turned up the music again. "You have to listen to your therapist."

It would be ten years before I'd try therapy again.

That Tuesday or Wednesday, there had been a school-wide memorial assembly: Celine's teachers, friends, and coaches giving tributes to her, the "girl who has been so cruelly taken from us." I hadn't had the guts to be there that day, or back to school at all.

Friends told me that, before the end of the assembly, a teacher stood from the crowd. This was a guy I barely knew and didn't very much like. He walked straight to the microphone. It was a surprise; the teacher hadn't been designated to speak.

"Along with the sadness," he said, taking the mic from the principal, "I know there's a lot of anger here." This teacher wasn't a hippie, but he was given to wearing pullover baja shirts in his social studies class and I'd laughed behind his back many times. "Great emotion is justified in tragic events like these. But we should take a second to remember that Darin is a student in the North Shore community, too." (Our school had about five hundred and twenty students total.) "The reports tell us he wasn't at fault, and I am sure we can agree he's a good person."

It was years before I wrote to thank him, this guy

I didn't really know, who was decent enough to perform a simple kindness, the kindness of remembering the young man whose well-being it would have been easy, at that moment, to forget. I didn't say a word to him the rest of my high-school days.

42

As I waited to decipher the forming pattern of accusations and consequences, I returned to class. It was early June, about a week after the accident and a few days before the funeral.

I was met at North Shore High's front door with a stormy look from Melanie Urquhart, one of Celine's friends. I had prepared for this, or something like it. What high-schooler wouldn't glare hard at the boy who killed her friend?

I had the hunch, as I contrived my way from class to cafeteria and back, that my day would be filled by these black glances. I was wrong. With frightened eyes, I looked everywhere, at everyone. And in the homerooms and corridors, there quickly grew around me a zone of silence and inviolability. Except when my friends would suddenly mount brief, haphazard campaigns of everything's normal, quoting lines from *Fletch* and slapping my book bag or calling me a dick.

All the same, the inescapability of what had happened—what was happening now as I showed my face in the clogged thoroughfare between classes—threw who I really was into shadow, even to myself. It felt somehow like living at the last limits of objective reality. I seemed less real than the plain, plump truth did. Because I'd driven a certain road, someone who had been alive was dead. I had killed someone. And yet, that wasn't the end of it. Because now the daily me was back: the residue of that accident returned to school. The shambling or smiling or lurking person who'd run down the girl. I remember the first time after the accident my name was called in class, the feel of pause and hush in the room, like deer scenting something strange. Everyone's ears and tails flicked. Speaking aloud here meant, all at once, that I was a student again. I'd have to work to be as present, as definable, as *real* as the accident was.

Before lunch, Jim—the guy who'd been such a jocular monster at the movie house—apologized and tried to explain himself. This was like that surprise tribute my social studies teacher had given at the assembly, a case of spot kindness. Jim was telling me that when we'd seen each other, he'd heard only that there'd been *some* kind of accident. And if he'd known that a person had actually been seriously *hurt,* let alone *died,* he of course wouldn't have ever dared or even *dreamed* of, etc. Who cared what he said; his hands were on my shoulder. He asked three or four times how I was, and his grip on my arm felt good. When he saw I couldn't answer, he'd interrupt my pauses. His nervous eyes watched me above his words, apologizing for the ways the excuses weren't right even as he couldn't stop presenting them.

Another buddy, Eric, assured me that he and others had started in on the high-school equivalent of push-polling, of caucusing for votes. *Come on,* they'd say to anyone still on the fence, the undecideds. *Wasn't it a little suspicious how she just* turned *into his car? You ever think of that?* To her friends they'd say quietly: *We have to be there for Darin, too. We have to support him, too.*

For all that, my inviolability zone wasn't airtight. An AP English teacher, rancorous and grim, squinted my way: I'm almost positive he shook his head and grumbled as we passed each other. But more often what happened was vague. Students in hallways passed looks back and forth, telling one another: Hey, go on tiptoes around a griever like this. Or they just shunned me—quickened their pace, hid their heads in open lockers. I got a sense of which look signified what. Grievers become connoisseurs of the averted eye. My stomach was wincing the entire week. Except now and then, on the second and third days, when a few non-friends dared talking to me. At those moments, there would be that echoed *thump!* everywhere in the chest.

On the off chance I would need to chat, I'd prepared a whole, verbatim pitch. ("The entire thing happened in like an eye blink.") When I delivered it, I'd see myself as poignantly sad, even a bit *aw-shucks,* with sundown lighting and uncertain piano tinkles right out of Hollywood, a scene trembling on the brink of discovery.

Again, most people steered clear, but a few—"Hey Darin, that morning did you have any, well, accidents happen, whatever—I'm sure you weren't, I mean, who gets *drunk* during the day, but I'm just asking, did you . . ."—a few kids did say things that demanded I address the accident. I'd chew off my monologue piece by piece, fussily clearing my throat, letting out a chunk at a time. It was the version I'd settled on, official and even true, but in a way that seemed to go against the spirit of truth: facts with edges sanded, corners rounded. ("Again, I didn't really see her cut in front of me until pretty much, you know, impact.")

The kids who did talk to me usually said: *Most of us understand it wasn't your fault,* or some other soft response. And I even got awarded this: in front of my locker, the football team captain face-gestured my way. (With, I should admit, infinite disinterest.) He was the physical king of the class; his nod played up his good chin, the charisma of his nose . . . But so what seemed to be happening to me was a surprise. I don't mean that North Shore High accepted my return with a gentle yawn. A fatal accident will remain a trusty motor of cafeteria scuttlebutt—I could intuit that as I humped around carrying my lunch tray. I felt like a paper cutout, poised there, being snipped into conversations at every table.

The school also had, of course, a few death fetishists. Kids who drew intricate pen-and-ink arabesques on their notebooks, who scratched BLACK SABBATH or ANTHRAX in their official fonts on the spine. These kids jostled over again and again, offering condolences but wanting accounts, details, details. I was a figure to them; to them, I may as well have been walking the halls with a black cowl and sickle. There was one girl in particular. She had mannish hair, cut in a greasy style. It was obvious, as she interrogated me—the wide eyes, the thrilled cheeks—that by talking about this, she felt close to something decayed and vibrant.

But still, what now seemed a qualified acceptance of me at NSHS came as a relief—compared to my own serfs-with-pitchforks visions. My reception exceeded what I'd hoped for. All the same, a new unease came shyly into my heart, as if on tiptoe. I didn't know what it was. And then I did.

By fifth period I could pretty well catalog the variety of reactions. Some misread my tense, android gloom as some Mahatma Gandhian state of moral insight or knowledge. (As if, via something like virtue osmosis, those who brush up to death just *arrive* at the sense of what matters and what does not.) Other kids (friends of Celine's and some basic misanthropes) flat-out blamed me for killing her, though this group mostly bit their tongues about it. But most people's reactions lacked all intensity. If you were neither a close friend nor some kind of rival, it was easier to give "the tragic event" a minute of incomprehension and then go about your adolescence. "This," I thought, "is *it*?"—someone has *died*. But the student body, stepping into summer sunlight, had grabbed its beach towel. It was nice out—that bright gush of weeks right before graduation—and your future rarely feels so present as it does in this June of your prime. The accident, to pretty much the whole school, was just one black feather in the larger scheme of things.

I didn't understand that everyone's tepid emotions were reasonable. The panicky little drum that kept me going required that this event, this death, be epochal. Of course, it *was* that: this was an incomprehensibly sad occurrence for our school, our town. But I didn't yet know that there are some truths—that even young people die occasionally; that there's only so much gnashing of teeth and weeping over another person's tragedy—there are some truths that only come to us softened by beautiful stratagems of self-deception. Nobody wants to be reminded. Nobody wants to hear the sad song again.

Melanie Urquhart, at the end of that first day, approached my locker. I braced myself: here it comes.

As she closed in—backpack straps, yellowish hair, eyes at my face—I realized I wanted to hear it. This is what I craved, the fullest force. The worst thing. I needed it to be spoken, and by someone outside of myself, so I could determine whether it was true. Melanie was short but took long, fast steps. Here was judgment, at last. One quirk that makes life hard—for the mobile packets of truth and lies we all are—is that we're all imprinted with a kind of bullshit meter. It's nonpartisan. It gauges what others say, and what we say, too. It's most active socially; it goes to sleep when we're just thinking. I felt a magnetic pull to Melanie now. I got excited, even brimming.

"I'm sorry, I—" she barely managed, "—*support* you." She told it straight to my sneaks.

It was insincere. Melanie had been peer-pressured into coming. "You're okay, Darin, which is important, too." She was talking with steep reluctance. Or maybe she meant everything she said. I don't know. It couldn't have been easy for her—or for any of my still-stunned classmates.

What I wanted to tell her was: "I'm sorry I haven't cried. I may not look it, but I'm overcome by this, a total mess, a wreck on two feet." I didn't say that—not that, or much of anything I can recall.

And so, as with the policeman in the newspaper, as with the Shrink, as with my decision to not even find out which hospital Celine had been in, I avoided the moment once again. The moment when I would be compelled to know what I felt about this.

When would the funeral be? The weekend—meaning not
tomorrow, or the day after, but on the far side of the week?
I mean, weren't they always on the weekend?

My father and I went to the funeral alone. I'm not sure why my mother didn't join us. It wasn't that I hadn't wanted her to. But as a family, we'd fallen into a set of dance steps: when calamity happened, Mom would stand off to the side, looking into her soda until someone would ask if she wanted to join in or not.[1]

When it comes to the funeral itself, my memory squints and mumbles.

At the church door I took a shaky gulp and wrapped my palms around the handles and my heart was a live bird nailed to my chest. Selfishness was thrumming at me: Don't open this door, just take off! Maybe it only *seems* like the right thing to do, showing up today, but probably mine is the last face her parents and friends and whoever wants to see, yes that's true maybe it only *appears* that the more mature thing

---

1. I should mention, if only in a footnote, how great my parents and sister were throughout this. Real difficulty, if it holds any benefits, holds this one: sometimes it lets you find out if your family has a genius for kindness, for devotion under pressure. In mentioning even this, however—merely giving my parents and sister their due—I feel again the weird twinning of my story with Celine's, a feeling of *how dare I mention my family at all*. The Zilkes must have faced a howling sadness that makes what my parents were dealing with seem completely inconsequential, just smoke and cobwebs.

is to open this door right now, but in fact the braver thing is maybe to *not* face it. I mean, I am the guy who drove the car and I'm showing up to her funeral? Are you serious about this? Because no one and I mean no one would expect you to have to, even if it is the manlier thing to do, or whatever, because you're not even a man yet really, etc.

My father stood at the door and showed no expression of any kind: it was up to me. I opened the door.

I bowed and averted through the crowd, I swallowed and hesitated. This was—and remains—the hardest thing I've ever had to do. But I was relieved to feel tears on my face. Among the selves jostling inside me was an actor who could manipulate people, while the frightened kid in there sweated out his confusion. Real tears, some part of me knew, were right. I wasn't fully aware of most of this: I felt so much but understood so little, could express so little. I greeted the wetness on my face with relief.

An old man clamped his eyes on me as if he wanted to cut my heart out. Imagine outliving not only your children, but your grandchildren. The man was frail, with the body—slim hips, short, a big belly—of a schoolgirl eight months into a mistake. He stood to the left of my path and didn't move; my father and I had to glide around him. His head revolved carefully, never releasing me from the grip of his gaze. I turned and looked—my father had, too—and the man kept staring.

(I now think tears don't mean anything so much as overload. You don't know *what* you feel. So tears spill out.)

I was bewildered and guilt-ridden and I hadn't even faced Celine's parents yet.

54

And then I did. Some mortician or other heartache functionary shunted me into a back-chamber where they were—it was like a green room for this particular death's celebrities. I tried, for some reason, not to cry here, as if *that* was what was expected of me. I was trying to act as a kind but hard-judging person would want me to act.

I had the child's faith that going through every official rite—psychiatry, returning to class—would restore me to an appropriate place in everyone's eyes. *Darin was brave enough to go to the funeral. He didn't duck, nor did he shirk. He did The Right Thing.* I hadn't realized that the hard-judging person was myself.

Celine's father, a big man, came to me with a surprisingly light step. He didn't know what to do with his face. It was soft and jowly, and he wore glasses that gave him a Tom Bosley, *Happy Days* aspect. This made me to think he'd be gentle and understanding.

In the long moment before he found words, and as he took my hand, Mr. Zilke settled on an expression, a hard-won glint of: *I will be friendlier than you have any right to expect me to be.*

"You're Darin."

My voice and my face behaved as if this were a regular meeting between cordial strangers. I was nervous about sounding nervous, and nervous about sounding anything but nervous. (Even now I feel my face go red as I remember this: having complicated her parents' grief with the question of how to treat me was perhaps the worst thing I could have done. A possibly brave act for me, but awful for them.)

Celine's mother joined us. (The thing is, I still don't know what would have been the right and respectful thing to do, other than having shown up.) I think her mother attempted a smile, but not a single muscle obeyed; she stood there exempt from all expression. Then her cheeks flared a difficult color. She was preparing to do something.

First, a clenching of her body, a steeling herself for something personally odious. She let out a noise: part sob and sigh, part venom. She hugged me quickly, and just as quickly shrank away.

"I know it was not your fault, Darin. They all tell me it was not your fault." She swallowed, and took me in with exhausted eyes. "But I want you to remember something. Whatever you do in your life, you have to do it twice as well now." Her voice went dim. "Because you are living it for two people." Her face was a picture of the misery that had worn out the voice. "Can you promise me? Promise."

Yes, of course, of course, Mrs. Zilke—and the accident churned my stomach. And here again came that reflector sliding up, like those raindrops on the Shrink's Porsche: up and over my windshield. But somehow it still didn't seem right to promise Mrs. Zilke this. How can you commit to something you don't even understand? Was I to become the Zilkes' son now, visiting on school breaks, calling in with news of grades and girls?

I tried to scrub my face of all emotion and message, to let Mrs. Zilke fill it with whatever meaning would bring her comfort.

"Can you promise me, Darin?" Her eyes got very hectic. "*Promise.* You're living for two. Okay? Okay?"

I nodded quickly.

And she continued to gaze at me. Not too unkindly or even severely, just for a long while. I swallowed what had become a big pointy stone in my throat. Some clock somewhere kept beating its subdued cymbal. I looked away and then back. She was still looking at me. *Why are you the one who is still alive?* her eyes seemed to be saying.

I opened my mouth to tell her—what? Nothing. Finally, at once, she turned to leave: she wanted, forever, to have no part of this life she'd doubly freighted. My dad leveled his hand on my back, on my shoulder. A kind of drape of family, holding me, recasting me as his, and our family's.

Next I'm standing before Celine's open coffin. I don't remember how I got here, who's brought me. I only remember the tingly awareness of the two hundred whispers at my back, and how that got every hair on my body to stand up. Celine looked almost like herself. What I mean is, she now looked more like her high-school self than she had when I'd mistaken her for someone pale and dozing on the road.

I haven't really described her appearance at all. Her face was soft and broad, pretty and unpretending. Pretty without being stagy about it.

Everybody wants life to speak to them with special kindness. Every personal story begs to be steered toward reverie, toward some relief from unpleasant truths: That you are a self, that beyond anything else you want the best for that self. That, if it is to be you or someone else, you need it to be you, no matter what. I'm not sure I can get across just how much I want to be extra-generous to Celine here. Extra-generous and, you've probably noticed, extra-writerly. It's a coward's tactic. I'm trying to write all the difficulty away.

What if I tell you it was windy when I fled the memorial, so that all the trees moaned in protest. Is that puffed up enough, labored and lyrical enough, to seem like something extracted from a novel—and not just a real day of a real boy and a real dead girl?

I want very badly to tell you Celine was unusually beautiful. *Celine was unusually beautiful.* And to equate her with quiet, sleeping Juliet—or some such overdone b.s. Will the tuneful balancing of q and t sounds—the thing I've learned to do with my life after Celine—isolate me from the reality of what happened? (Which was merely this: here was a plainly attractive and nice girl I kind of knew who died after she pedaled into my car.)

The truth is—if I even have access to the truth—I remember Celine only with certain key words: athletic, broad face, good-natured, bicycle. These words call up no images. Real memory is a mix of blast and keepsake. For me, with this event, there is nothing—at least not in the part of the brain I live in. My mind looks away. I see only letters on a page, vowels and consonants, press and flop. There: I'm still trying to write and write and write away the reflector. . . .

So I can't share the image of what lay inside the coffin.

I don't have enough mental steam to make it all the way there.

What I do remember is self-centered—my own turning from the casket. I'm hurrying past all the stares in this neat and unreal spectacle. The heels of my unfamiliar dress shoes clack on the church floor. My stomach has been clutched and empty all morning; it's already been a long, hungry day. Soon enough I'm spluttering past the old grandfather, almost at the exit. And my dad keeps buzzing in my ear, "Keep your head up; just keep your head up . . ." The grandfather's head is dropped so he won't have to bear the sight of me.

I hadn't realized I'd been slouching my own head. I felt buoyed by an almost infant-level admiration for my father, and I wondered if I would ever know the things grown-ups know. I lifted my head.

Looking back now, there's something that bothers me about the newspaper article about her death: it has Celine as Knockout, as Queen Bee, as Prom Superstar. The kid the newspaper grieved for wasn't Celine. She was none of those things. Their version of her was less distinctive than the real Celine was, less an individual, devoid of any real-life individual's quirks and smudges. The paper seemed to believe Celine's death could only be fully newsworthy, only fully sad, if she were outlandishly beautiful, outlandishly popular, outlandishly everything.

The gym was an over-lit expanse of mascot banners, fluttery clothes, gaudy streamers, flashing cameras, graduation kitsch. NSHS was dressed for an end-of-year assembly. (This wasn't graduation, per se; just the entire school, flippant and free, enjoying a practice run/celebration.) But as soon as the proceedings got on their feet, the principal decided to take a moment. She started launching into—and my stomach clutched; I knew what was coming—a sermon about Celine's death.

Hundreds turned, a mass, bovine shift: this was the school's first sanctioned, public mention of Celine in front of me. How would I react? Warm-faced, I focused hard on my thighs.

"I want to just take a little time here to talk about creating a Celine Zilke memorial scholarship." The principal's voice staggered, recovered. My lap looked pretty much the way it always did.

"Planning's begun on this scholarship for next year," the principal said, "to I think be a really appropriate way in which to say goodbye."

She touched her birdnesty hair and cleared her throat, and now even *she* was looking in my direction. I was the unpredictable quantity this morning: the bomb that might blow, the sparked fuse.

My inviolability zone was gone. What would happen now?

"As you all are aware," the principal was saying, "the worst thing that can happen to a class happened to the Class of 1989 . . ."

Every time I circled away from some kid who sat gawking at me (pimply James Harmon, round Mark Reiniger), I'd catch another stare, and another.

Meantime, the speech inched ahead. A lot of sentiment and intensity, but a kind of murk when it came to purpose and message. An official speech.

"This is the exact sort of tragedy that is so difficult for a town to get over . . ." the principal said (or something very like this).

A cluster of helium balloons on the ceiling left tinted shadows on large-haired girls in sleeveless denim, on jocks and druggies, on some mats piled in a corner, on preppies in tennis outfits, on flannel shirts rolled to the elbow; over hoisted basketball hoops and the intelligent faces of my own anxious clique. It seemed like the *Sgt. Pepper's* cover. I was pelted by the storm of color and variety. I was sitting freely among the student body. No one had stopped me.

"A disaster of this magnitude," the principal was narrowing her eyes at a note card, "makes us look ahead and how we can strengthen this community using our shared values . . ."

Some crude engine of self-preservation revved up in me. "Um," I whispered. "I think, um." I was presenting total emotional vulnerability: a calculated decision. "Um, I think—"

Now, I felt no sadder at this particular moment than I'd felt during any recent other ones. (I had been constantly hurting.) But I felt oversized and bright again, spilling glow on people. I needed everyone to see that this—not just the death, but all this silent judgment, plus the stroke of our principal having given this speech in front of me—I needed everyone to see that it all touched me, too. I needed this for a simple reason: If I were able just to sit here and take it, I'd have been a monster in their final memories of me.

"Many of us have stories about Celine, so many wonderful and inspiring and . . ."

So here was another ritual. As in all rituals, people had expectations about how it should be performed. It was as if every moment at which I could have expressed my real sense of what had happened—my anxiety, confusion, queasy guilt; the Houdini sensation that everyone who escapes blame feels, everyone who has been pronounced blameless—they all worked to obstruct that sense. It was blocked off by a completely different sense, that of other people watching me.

"Excuse me," I said. I said, "I've got to get out."

And with each ritual performed successfully, another wall came up between me and the people I might have gone to and said: I don't know how to feel about this. Because if I admitted that, it would mean my public self had been a lie, and that lie would become their lasting thought of who I was.

"Excuse me, please."

I pushed through the crowd, which had turned startled and buzzing. I wasn't really any more inconsolable than a ham in a refrigerated case. Dumb pink meat.

"Excuse me, please," I said, with my pre-averted eyes. "Just need to get, um."

Where was I going? This seemed new—this slow, vile feeling of complaisance. (Although I suppose there isn't much progress in a personality: I'd done pretty much the same act for those girls I'd met at the accident site, when I'd slipped to my knees. Those girls had wanted some absolute image of guilt, and I'd matched up with every public presentation of large responsibility we'd all ever seen.)

Now I wanted the gym to note the impressiveness of my fighting off tears. Inside the shadows of my own life, I was *still* fumbling around to feel, in a genuine way, my role. (Even the final "um" was deliberate. It felt, in my throat and mouth, sappy.)

At last I got away. I was alone.

Outside the gym door, sunshine after a rain. Dew winking on grass, the parking lot looking scrubbed and raked, sun clipping off car tops, bright sky reflected in pools on roofs and tennis courts. At the edge of it all, there was a large maple—water stuck in a hundred leaves—having a private rainstorm.

I stood and watched and felt pleasantly without audience. Wind collected in my shirt at the armpits and feathered through the hair in front of my ears. I saw geese honk by and heard the leathery muscular flutter of their wings.

How hard these birds work to get aloft! I'd never thought about this before. And all around, the pepper-and-grass smell of a clean world after rain.

It was only after a moment that I realized my friends Eric and Jim (Jim, the movie-line cut-up) had come to join me out by the back fields. My escape from the gym—from its collective, frowning expression—wasn't *just* cynical and vain. Removing the distraction of myself had been, in part, a considerate act. Or my idea of considerate. Now the event could continue, as if Celine had been killed not by my car, but by a lamppost or a tree. That is to say, killed not by a classmate, but by one of the world's hard, inarguable stops. That's how it seemed, at least, in the bop and echo chamber between my ears. And I appreciated that my friends were here, that they'd shuffled after me outside. If I'm remembering right, we didn't say anything. Outside the school, I felt no need to cry, even to pretend. I had the jitters you get when you sense you've pulled a fast one. That was in there, too. But what exactly had I pulled, and on whom? I kept churning from mood to mood. The fact that it really *had* been impossible for me to sit in that gym and hear about Celine's death—this hadn't occurred to me. Eric, anyway, had also caught the jitters. His shiny face, when I glanced to the side, showed the tender curl of smile on his top lip.

So my friends and I just hung out for a while, tumbling quietly through the new uncertainty of things. The coming graduation; leave-taking; the world beyond us damp and sunny and waiting for our entrance. I thought that having fled a high-school gym with the selfishness of a coward just because someone's name is mentioned (and because yours isn't) maybe didn't meet all requirements of living your life valiantly for two people. I thought how unlucky it was that, of all the kids in this school, of the five carloads of people who had witnessed the accident—of all the possible others in Long Island—*I'd* been the one who'd had some girl's bicycle swerve left into his car. It was the obvious thought, and the first time I'd really felt it. And I thought with uncomplicated gratitude how strange and fortunate it was that I still had a life. I thought what it might mean not to have a life. (I didn't get very far on that one. What could it mean? It was absence: what was Celine not experiencing, not thinking about, not planning?) I thought I would powerfully if gradually rise above despair. I thought maybe I still didn't feel the right amount of despair. I thought how do you calculate a sum like that? I thought about unrealized lives. I thought Celine's parents were both probably home right now, not working on this workday. I thought, Who was I kidding, I'll never get over this. Or maybe her parents *had* had to go back to work already, and was that the sadder thing, life forcing you to just go on? I thought how vacant and baggy their house must seem. I remembered my house the day I'd stayed away from school: so moonscape empty. I thought of a house seeming that way all the time, breeze slanting in under the bottoms of windows, carrying warm leaf smells and tarmac-and-exhaust smells, sun on floors and corners and tables. And there also, the undeniable emptiness, the silence on everything, that want of familiar noises—of another creature's set of noises.

Eric peeked back inside the gym to see the principal finish up her talk. Then we reinserted ourselves into the crowd. Oh, look at *this*: Darin's back. I was a piece of living trivia. The balloons, that broad squeaking heaven, still floated overhead. I took my seat, the ceremony went on, etc.

About two weeks later, I graduated and left town.[2]

I saw college as a type of witness-protection program. I was so eager for the fresh identity, I'd get sweaty thinking about it. Everyone in my high school knew. No one at Tufts did, and while I was there they never would.

But I did make one important stop in town before I left: Celine Zilke's parents' house. At the funeral, they'd invited me to "come by whenever," so I thought I owed them a visit. I thought they expected this, even wanted it. How I thought about Celine was in large part still governed by conformity, by appearances: if I didn't know exactly how

---

2. Before that, though—before graduation, the prom. I'd been set to take a girl from another town. She and I'd been orbiting each other like nervous rabbits, but hadn't made it even to the make-out stage. Now, though, after the accident transpired—after my name appeared in the newspaper—it was over. I hadn't thought she'd have even heard about the crash. Wrong. "I'm not going to go with you anymore," she said, hurriedly removing herself from me and this book. I was pretty intent, all the same, on showing my face at prom. ("The accident hasn't wrecked me totally; the accident hasn't wrecked me totally . . .") Smiles can be little contentment generators: when you pretend to feel a few clicks better than you really are, you actually get some small upturn in your mood. That's what I'd been hoping, anyway. And I caught a break: my sweet and lovely date from last year's junior prom was, improbably, still free for this one, too. She was kind enough to go with me. And so I went to the prom. The end.

I *was,* I could at least control how I *seemed,* and seeming was where all benefit lay.

I went to the Zilkes' alone. I actually imagined a cozy welcome. They'd smile, maybe touch my cheek, we'd cry together.

I knocked. And when I knocked—when my bunched hand hit Celine's real door—I realized this may have been a mistake. My stomach shuddered up toward my throat. Maybe nobody's home? I leaned an ear to the wood, made out the clumps and risings of voices. After a courage-building swallow, I knocked again. One man's voice got louder and more distinct, coming closer. The door opened. It was Celine Zilke's father.

After seeing me, Mr. Zilke turned back to the room: "Oh, look who it is." I had a good view of the back of his head. "It's Darin." He said this as if he was proud I'd showed. As if he'd that very instant been defending me.

"He's here to say how sorry he is," he told the room— really grinding the knuckle of his emotion into the words. "To *apol*ogize." This was a few days after the funeral.

"Hello," I said, smiling in a queasy way.

It was afternoon, and there were five or six other people around, collected in the Zilkes' den—family members, fellow grievers, people I didn't know. Pressing into the room (and it felt like a programmed momentum that carried me, not the normal mechanics of foot and leg) had the spooky feel of straining against a gravitational force. Everyone kept their mouths shut with such fervor they seemed lipless.

There was the smell of stale coffee. *Was* I here to apologize? The Zilkes had said at the funeral that they knew it wasn't my fault, hadn't they? Did they somehow miss the *Newsday* article? I had the abrupt-swerve, waking-nightmare sense that I'd gotten it wrong, that I'd imagined the newspaper entirely.

Mr. Zilke guided me to the couch. His hand, when I shook it, had a really human clamminess. Then he left for the kitchen, came back, offered me a tall iced tea. He put a coaster down.

"How are you?" I said, stupidly.

"Okay," he said. "Yes. You know."

"Good," I said—taking a very long sip and swallowing before finally lowering my glass to the coaster. Then that was finished.

Mr. Zilke could not keep focused on me. The quiet now was that kind where the only sounds are domestic ones: a far-off refrigerator, acorns clanking onto a drainpipe. Nobody moved. My arrival had strained this place; you could still feel a twang in the air. The thing Mr. Zilke *could* keep focused on stood behind my iced-tea glass—a picture of Celine in a shiny frame.

The visit was a promise kept too soon, a handshake attempted in the dark and made with the wrong person. They didn't want me here and I didn't want to be here. After a few more minutes, Mr. Zilke shepherded me to the door.

Under the lintel, he rested an almost narcotized stare on

me—tilting his face, squeezing his lip with two fingers—as if sussing out a faint noise in the house, a neighboring yard, a far-off country.

"No matter what," he said finally, "we would never blame you, Darin."

Past his shoulder, I watched the other guests exchange *Well, that's that* looks. I drifted back to my car with the cold sensation of a type of social death—the small certainty you get on a few occasions in your life, when a parting has no assurance of a return. I would never, I was sure, see the Zilkes again.

Five months later, I learned that Celine's parents were suing me for millions of dollars.

2

"An accident isn't necessarily ever over."
                                        —Diane Williams

At college, I spent a lot of my first year with physics and psychology books, gulping down studies and figures. I took solace in math: you're doing forty, and the girl with the bicycle cuts ten feet in front of you—impact will arrive in something like 700 milliseconds. Human perception time—not only to see a hazard, but to understand one as such—is generally accepted to saw off some 220 milliseconds. Next, the mostly neural job of getting foot to brake demanded another 500 milliseconds. It seemed I was exculpated by 20 milliseconds.

These numbers I sought in the library. There was a pattern: sometimes when I sat bucketed in an easy chair, or studied coursework in my lap, I'd tell myself it was time for a washroom break or something. But then I'd find myself in the physical-science stacks, my fingers tapping over books, making sure that my reassuring numbers were still there, that they were still reassuring.

It was always the same, even before I knew I was being sued. It took about forty minutes and then I would end up on my feet—placemarking my textbook, leaving it in the cushions, and shambling off. One time I passed a friend who was going through microfiche—the old whir of newspapers, the blue of ink and gray flashing in front of her head—and I began to tear up, out of panic. Because the library was double-edged. It had my relief in it and my guilt: my physics numbers in the upstairs collections, and, down by periodicals, the record of me and Celine. Had my friend found out, was she searching for me in a Long Island tabloid?

I *still* didn't know that legal threats were gathering, attempts at authorized ruin, cold winds from home. Regardless, I was thinking about Celine as often as ever. I internalized my cares about conventionality and appearances.

The moments before the crash became a kind of VHS tape, over-rented, overplayed, stripped: the colors scratched away, the sound wobbly—until I didn't try to remember at all, and the tape would burst into high-def vividness. Hair, bicycle, reflector. I'd be doing something mundane, like removing a soda from an icy case at the Mini Mart. And while my fingers closed around the damp, solid aluminum, I would think: *Celine Zilke will never feel a can in her grip again*. I was also muddling through the soundstage brightness of occasional flashback. I'd rush to class, take a corner, look at some kids hackey-sacking on the quad and see the gross anatomy of a bicycle lying in the street. Or Celine's glassy face.

It never occurred to me to petition for antidepressants or sign myself in for another psychotherapy go-round. I knew what was troubling me. Depression as a chemical shortcoming, a chronic formless mope, could be handled: a pill could gather it and sink it down its hole. But for what seemed an

appropriate response to a problem that couldn't be fixed—
that sort of depression struck me as without cure.

And without much choice, I made sure that another
potential cure wasn't available. No friend could cheer me,
could talk me out of anything. The people I lived with and
ate with at college didn't know. No one who encountered
me in classrooms, at a frat party, in the campus center, noticed the fierce inner battles I'd fought to make the different
Darins into a Darin that friends could recognize. Coming
back to my room, I always worked up a cheerful face—
abstracted but busy. What if someone had said, "Hey, is
something wrong?"

I didn't know the right answer, and didn't have confidence in how I'd respond.

So I quietly indulged in the self-pity that, in the vener-
able tradition of sad people everywhere, I felt entitled to.

I began college under-read. Bookishness, rigorous thought, affection for time-consuming study—my public high school hadn't prepared me for any of it. Besides, until Celine I'd been a lazy student, an underachiever. But somehow freshman year, a faked understanding—a rarefied reference, a split-second attempt to scale the tower—got me through. Oh yes, that's *so* right, and wasn't it Kafka who said . . . ? Gibberish, bullshit. But I felt I had to look smart enough for two. (Not necessarily to *be* smart enough. It was still largely about appearances, still largely social.)

Freshman year, I took a "Death & Dying" class. Generous helpings of Elisabeth Kübler-Ross, side plates of *When Bad Things Happen to Good People,* and other softbrained texts—solemn, whispering titles like "Meditations." I believed I could depend on a professor–student privilege, so I went ahead and wrote my midterm about the accident. A lot of the coursebooks had line-drawn covers showing pine trees or lonely outcroppings of rocks. The grad student who ran this touchy-feely seminar urged me to nose around, to "check out Celine's side of things."

I thought nosing around was a terrible idea. (*Everybody can master a grief but those who have it* was a Shakespeare line I circled during a survey class.) But I was an obedient student. I had become, after leaving Glen Head, accommodating of any rule; I'd had to become less like a chance-taker who might have once been involved in an accident.

So I falteringly did what the grad student had asked. I grubbed up addresses, wrote letters, rooted out old phone numbers, butted into lives: the other bicyclist from that morning, a girl Celine had played field hockey with, a chem-lab partner—anyone I could trace down from her world.

I learned that Celine had remade herself in the months before her death. She had become a born-again. And once I found my way to her field-hockey friend, I discovered something that for years changed how I felt about Celine's death.

Our phone chat was short and intense:

"I'm really really sorry to call like this. Because, well—" Immediately I was thrashing around. Talking too fast, explaining too much. "Because I sort of, I'm taking this class and need to find out more about, you know, *her*. Because of the class and the class leaders thought one really helpful thing might be to—"

"Wasn't that diary thing weird?" the girl said.

What diary thing?

"Oh," the girl said. She'd overstepped. "I guess I assumed you knew."

I could feel my heart, its sudden and loud *lubdub,* blood lurching through the aorta.

"So you don't know?" she said.

Celine had written, right before the crash, something to the effect of: "Today I realized that I am going to die." It had been her mother who told this field-hockey friend about it.

"Thank you," I said, and hung up. I may even have said it again, after laying the phone down. It was like a pressure along every part of my body had been snipped away: cut ropes flinging out crazily, weights tumbling from arms, shoulders, head. *Today I realized that I am going to die.* They were just eight words. I'd already grabbed them for dear life.

Celine, I decided, had died on purpose. That's why she'd turned right in front of my car. (From what I understood, her family hadn't been much invested in religion, and that's why that born-again stuff not only came as a surprise, but actually had struck me as dispositive, somehow.) For me, the suicide note—or, rather, the hypothetically suicidal journal entry—settled it.

The first trial deposition came when I'd been away at college for a month. I caught a Greyhound home, and then Dad and I ambled over to the Nassau County courthouse, positive that this whole thing was a formality, that the Zilkes hadn't really decided to come after me. That they still maintained—as everyone did—I wasn't at fault.

(I don't know how the letter summoning me to the courthouse wasn't a dead giveaway. I guess that's how naïve I was.)

At the courthouse, Dad and I met the lawyer my insurance company had detailed to us: curly hair, wireframe glasses. This was on Mineola's Franklin Avenue, behind a grove of telephone poles. The lawyer and I shook hands, and above his soft grip his face was pale and serious. This was not the face of mere formality. As he hurried us down the lobby (lights and footsteps spanking off the marble floor), he told me I was being "litigated against." Wait, the Zilkes are *coming after* me? In the flurry of information, I didn't catch the guy's name. Why would they sue me, after their promise? It wasn't until the elevator doors shut that I felt control over my features and bodily functions return.

My dad and I followed the lawyer into a room in the

lower floors. And here the lawyer divulged the cruel, galactic sum the Zilkes could get from me if the trial went horribly wrong. (It was beyond what the insurance company even covered; it was more money, I was sure, than I would ever have.) The low-ceilinged place we entered was called a Special Hearings room. I had to recalibrate myself again: Mr. Zilke sat about ten feet from me.

All at once I could see him bringing me that iced tea in his front room. And now he wouldn't look me in the eye.

I'd imagined this deposition would take place in a judge's cozy chambers—polished wooden desk; a sort of brass-based, green, *LA Law*–ish lamp. Instead we'd all sidled one-by-one into this chalky and hideously lit sub-basementy place. A long plastic table commandeered most of the room.

"You okay?" my father asked me.

"Yeah," I said. I raised my chin, spoke confidently, and meant it. *"Yes."*

And as fast as that, under the burnished presence of a judge, the event began. Right away the Zilkes' lawyer trained his expertise on me. *How far did her body fly?*

Before I opened my mouth, I realized the confidence had been a bluff, a kind of performance for my father and myself, too. It was the weighted bat you swing bravely in the on-deck circle, which can't stop your knees from buckling when you step up to the plate.

How much did your car skid on the grass of the median before it came to a stop? With a hunter's eye, the Zilkes' lawyer targeted small rifts in my self-assurance and certainty. *Five cars around, why did she turn into* yours?

The lawyer flexed his eyebrows as he spoke—eyebrows that didn't believe me, that were already garnishing wages, spending the balance of a salary I hadn't earned yet.

"I don't know," I said.

Over and again, question after question. "Don't know. Not sure." I looked at my father for solace. This wasn't anything we'd expected. All he could do was watch me. Mr. Zilke, of course (there was a great deal of intensity at the table), saw that I was looking to my father.

"I don't know," I said, each time more softly than the last. "I don't know."

"What *do* you know?"

Then the Zilkes' lawyer inhaled through his nose and shut his eyes, slowly. A man visibly calming himself.

He came back from his settle-down place and continued. His style was a kind of word fog in which I couldn't make out any detail, only the growing sense of being lost and wrong: "What's the exact amount of seconds, son, between when you saw her and you killed her with your car? Because, right now, it doesn't *seem* like, with your answers—or lack of answers—there's any, shall we say, it's just that you strike me as someone who might be telling less than the fullest extent of the truth. Do you follow me?"

He searched my eyes, and for a moment, I got to search his. I made out, to my surprise, what looked like regret. Something shaky in the face, there in the spry brows—

a remorse about the power and edge that experience has over anxiety and weakness. (This was my thinking then.) "Take your time, son," he said.

In any court setting, where people have nothing to do but lean forward and listen, silences feel drawn-out. They convey an impression of somebody using the shade of a few extra moments to put together a hasty lie. I wasn't going to lie, though; I just didn't want to give the only answer I had. But now their lawyer's eyebrows hiked up as he waited for me to answer. My lawyer's did, too. I probably had no choice but to hand over my one skimpy truth. Even Dad's eyebrows were starting to pyramid. It seemed so artificial, somehow, that I couldn't simply step out from behind this table and head off into the telephone-pole orchard out there on Franklin Avenue.

"I don't *know* how many, exactly," I said. My face and the room seemed to be the same smarting temperature. Someone's chair leg scraped against the floor. And the Zilkes' lawyer, resetting himself, sat waiting for more.

"One second?" I said—a guessing game. "Half of one?" I was lucky I didn't just fall thwap onto the floor.

"So which, then?" the lawyer said. "One second or half? We're all here to listen to what you have to say."

Mr. Zilke, meanwhile, was bashful with his gaze until it failed him; he turned from the questioning and kept his eyes on his watch, on his cuffs. (Mrs. Zilke, like my own mother, wasn't there.)

More questions for me. *Were you drunk?* The Zilkes'

lawyer had the structural design of a Saint Bernard, sags and weight and flaccidity. *Can you prove you weren't drunk?*

(He'd later ask a policeman who'd been at the accident similar questions. Q: "How can you be sure young Mr. Strauss wasn't drunk?" A: "I've been a police officer for years. He wasn't drunk. I could tell." Q: "Were you derelict in your duty in not giving him a breathalyzer?" Etc.)

"Mr. Vancini, approach, please," the judge said, interrupting. Robed in the prestige of the state, he was the one relaxed figure in the room. The judge leaned forward to whisper something. Without ever having been in a court (or a Special Hearings room), I realized I knew the ins and outs of this place—lawyers approaching the bench; my having made the official promise to tell the truth; direct and cross and redirect examinations—just as everyone in the country did: from TV. Which is to say in my bones.

(Weeks later, when I got to see the court reporter's transcript, I read what the judge had actually murmured to the Zilkes' lawyer. "Mr. Vancini," he had said, "we all know how fond of money you are. If you don't stop badgering this young man, I will take some money from you, via a fine.")

During a break, I headed alone down the courthouse hallway to get a Coke. Teenage housewives and their husband-tyrants; a napper hogging the whole bench outside a courtroom; pre-divorce couples irreconciling their differences publicly; facial bruises; some lawyer yelling drill-sergeantly loud commands at his client; a professional witness checking something in a briefcase, preparing to testify for show and profit; teary faces, tattooed faces; a weeping thug and his parents against a wall; crying millionaires; one defendant poking her court-appointed attorney on the lapel. A whole different division of a city had been ousted and massed here. At least that's how I remember it: the complete anthology of anxieties. And I was here, too, however I looked to these people, holding my plastic Coca-Cola bottle—a kind of affiliation with the bright and normal world—a few inches ahead of my body, like a lantern. All these people: all of our lives were in doubt.

Back in the Special Hearings room, the deposition quickly ran its course. A few more vague yes-or-no questions. Then: all righty, thank you, goodbye. Nothing would be decided this morning.

On his way to the door, Dad stopped in front of Celine's father. (They'd met only at Celine's funeral.) I was afraid for a moment that Dad intended to punch him.

"He's a prince, this guy," Dad told our insurance company's lawyer, and smiled warmly.

This was not sarcasm. Dad grinned and patted Mr. Zilke's shoulder. This was nervousness, forced joviality. Emotion pressed a dark horizontal wrinkle across Mr. Zilke's scalp. But with forced appreciation, Mr. Zilke said hi and thank you. It was all very strange. Mr. Zilke's eyes were dry. He was taller than I'd remembered. The Zilkes' lawyer turned to me with his fat, meaningless face. Everyone left.

Driving home, I asked Dad: "So, listen, why'd you do that? I mean, a *prince*?"

"I don't know," Dad said. His hands tightened on the steering wheel. Dad couldn't tamp down, or maybe didn't even know about, his smile. "I guess I didn't have any idea what to say. It was like, I almost forgot he was suing us for a second. I remembered how nice he'd been at the funeral."

Being friendly to Mr. Zilke felt, somehow, very natural. Back at college, I needed to act that way, too. My thoughts about Celine now were about honoring her memory, however privately. Every time I thought of Celine's parents blaming me for the death they'd promised to absolve me of, I felt tender toward them.

But when I speculated that maybe they *didn't* blame me, but instead were just trying to wreck my life for money—or that maybe they were simply and totally ruined, which made them not even quite know what they were doing—at those times I'd orbit around my sadness and guilt, and agonize. Mr. Zilke had brought me iced tea in a room where—for the first time, among adults— I knew I was hated.

I did not blame them for suing me. I pictured the Zilkes standing over Celine in some awful white hospital room just before their daughter died. The father with the terrible pinch of loss in his mouth, trying to will Celine to wake up, to somehow go back and say *Be careful* and *Look both ways.* The mother gently squeezing the bumps of Celine's feet under hospital covers. Or wanting to get up from the bedside chair and stretch but being afraid to move. I saw her parents conferring together over the bleakest decisions, signing forms, crying, working not to look upset—because wasn't there maybe an off chance that Celine could perceive their sadness, or their fear? Mr. Zilke palming smooth the rumples in his dying daughter's bedding. How could anyone blame these people for anything?

Amy Hempel has a story, "In the Cemetery Where Al Jolson Is Buried." I read it a few years after college, and then read it again from the beginning immediately after I'd finished. Early and in passing, the narrator tells a very sick friend about a chimp whom someone had taught sign language. The story doesn't analyze sadness so much as prod it and poke at it. Near the end, the sick friend dies and the story goes out like this, once the narrator is left alone:

> I think [back to] the chimp, the one with the talking hands.
>
> In the course of the experiment, that chimp had a baby. Imagine how her trainers must have thrilled when the mother, without prompting, began to sign to her newborn.
>
> Baby, drink milk.
>
> Baby, play ball.
>
> And when the baby died, the mother stood over the body, her wrinkled hands moving with animal grace, forming again and again the words: Baby, come hug, Baby, come hug, fluent now in the language of grief.

3

"Bear your griefs yourself . . ."
—*As You Like It*

For years, the court case just dragged its slow length along. Nothing lawsuit-related would be going on, then I'd get word of a coming deposition—which then for some reason would be postponed, indefinitely. It seemed random, like when a dark sky decides not to rain. But even as our case would disappear around a corner, I could sense it wending its way—spreading its shadow, big and cold, inside the parts of me where Celine still was.

My old friend Jim attended Boston University, not far from Tufts. I could talk accident stuff to Jim, because he already knew. It was a bit of social math; I couldn't lose anything by it, because the crash already shaped how he saw me.

All the same, I talked to him about it exactly once.

Sophomore year and Christmastime. I was nineteen. Jim and I waited together at Logan airport for a flight home. I admitted, or tried to admit, that the painful fact of Celine's parents being out there, someplace, just seething, hating me, blaming me for their daughter's death, made me just . . . made me just . . .

How could I put words to the thick, gloomy *thing* that covered my mind—this nullity that even all these years later, when I call up that airport confession, makes it all play a little extra darkly in my brain's theater? This was the same pain, the same whole-soul despair, that got me thinking—mainly theoretically, in an informal way—about committing suicide.

I felt in contact with the Zilkes' hate, a long-distance communication between us, like a dispatch sent over telephone wire: a future, a jinx, message received. This silent communication with the Zilkes felt like the truest words anyone had said to me since the accident. The only unmuffled thing—what I'd waited to hear the whole time. *You did this. You alone are responsible.*

I didn't cry when talking about this to Jim. I just felt very, very sad. Tears came quickly and readily at movies—even the dumbest movies—and at commercials. (Even the most obvious: family gatherings, a new mayonnaise sampled at an outdoor table, or an affordable phone service—and I found myself reaching for the Kleenex. A man and woman taking each other's arms after leaving an especially understanding slow-motion bank, walking down a moody, populated street with smiles on their faces, and I was a puddle.) But I never cried about things in my own life. They seemed too small. And I never cried about Celine.

Jim listened carefully as I chattered on about the Zilkes. Holiday passengers circulated around, their belongings on stands and wheels: the flustered, the ardent, the frowning, the greeters and the greeted, the intersections of lives and plans at an airport.

"What dicks they are," Jim said.

My thought was—*no!* "I think her parents just don't have any idea what to do," I said. How would *he* act in their place?

Jim shook his head no. He put his hand on my biceps; I could feel the fingers through the wool. College was teaching all of us not to be so shy about touching, that contact was what adults did more of than children.

"Darin, dude, everyone knows how you feel. Don't beat yourself up. Her parents are already willing to beat you up for you," he said. "Those dicks."

I gave a small, gutless laugh and changed the subject. I very badly wanted to stand up for the Zilkes but didn't even try.

And then I was twenty and not talking about it at all, not even to people like Jim. That year I remember as one peeled of emotion. I didn't identify with the Zilkes' anger anymore. I really wasn't feeling at all, just finishing classes, closing books and subjects forever.

I belonged to no support groups, but still I somehow fell into the *serenity now* traps of rationalization and cop-out. It was easy to do. I had, of course, that journal entry. I think we all build superstructures in our heads, catwalks and trestles that lead us from the acceptance of our own responsibility to the cool mechanics of the factory, where things are an interlocking mess, where everybody's pretty much unaccountable. To be alive is to find a way to blame someone else.

At twenty-one I was studying in London, where avoidance was even easier. An ocean between me and the person who had done this.

Turning up a collar to Leicester Square fog, swigging one-pound lagers in fireplace pubs—these were just a very few of the uncountable experiences that Celine would never have. Every time I realized this (which was often) it came as a numbness that seemed to match the London weather: as though Celine was merely some girl I'd vaguely known in high school with very bad luck. I remember walking alone down British streets that directed everyone to Look Right, Look Left. This simple pavement advisory struck me, for pretty obvious reasons, as buzzing with whole realms of meaning.

The lawsuit still loomed over me. But I had Celine's journal entry. I relied on assumptions I made about it. The assumptions seemed burnished and solid, and I wouldn't have gotten through life without them.

And now I was at the end of my early twenties, spending a year in Colorado, moving to Manhattan. A different city than Boston or London, and certainly there was a much higher voltage to New York than you feel on Long Island— even just walking around the giant metal forest in whose shadow we all lived. The strangest thing about coming to Manhattan after a life in the suburbs: it's never really dark outside. Not ever. At any hour, there are lights in the street, cars on the road, a window bright with a person moving sleepily inside—changing a TV station, sitting down to a computer with a coffee. No matter what you're doing in New York you're not the only one, and the absurdity is that this movement and buzz makes you feel especially anonymous. People living too close to and too far from one another at the same time. As it was with me. Because I still told nobody, who really knew me here? How would I find out who else was like me?

My accident was the deepest part of my life, and the second-deepest was hiding it. This meant certain extra steps. Never introducing high-school friends to new friends. Never taking anyone home to Long Island. (I didn't want my parents to learn what I still felt about the crash—and I didn't know *what* it was that I felt, whether it was shame or guilt or anger. Plus, asking my family not to mention it would have started a conversation that would have left them puzzled and sad. I'm not sure if this will make sense to most readers. I think each family has a funhouse logic all its own, and in that distortion, in that delusion, all behavior can seem both perfectly normal and crazy.)

By now, the camouflage had become my skin. My friends wouldn't want to know. Who would want to know? I certainly didn't want to know. All I wanted was to hold my assumptions to the light, and to watch them sparkle in their facets, as all sham gemstones do.

Through all this, there was the courthouse threat of financial devastation—a thief taking up ominous position outside every job, every apartment, rubbing his hands together. Everything could at any moment be taken away because of the Zilkes, snatched from under me, desks pulled from my fingers. Her parents had found a very real way, I realized, to keep Celine with me forever.

During the gulp and wait of litigation, my distress sprouted a few surprising offshoots. I found the idea of people mistakenly thinking ill of me impossible to take. (This misunderstanding-phobia went even for your standard sitcom mix-up: if Diane incorrectly thought Sam did something wrong, I couldn't bear it and often left the room.)

The accident had also turned me squishily obliging. I always cozied up to people—so that if they ever learned the story, they'd say: "He seems so decent and kind. How awful that such a thing would happen to him!"

I never really got to know my insurance attorney; I watched him grow older at wide intervals, like a frame-advance special effect. The case seemed to have stalled. He was now in his late thirties, when time begins to do heavier work on you. I was living in that jittery meantime where an accused can almost mistake bureaucracy for reprieve, where it's possible to hope officials have simply misplaced the proper forms, let their attention wander, have clean forgotten. I kept this hope going. And then one evening it shattered against the blunt force of a lawyer's phone call.

But before I get into that, I should explain in greater specificity how the trial had actually started.

In May or June 1988, right after the crash, my insurer —more or less satisfied that no jury was likely to find me negligent—had followed an industry-wide policy of offering "the deceased's family" what insurers (charmingly) call "go-away money." In fatality accidents, this is the minimum a company will release: a careful figure above what it believes a plaintiff might be likely to gain in court, but below the hassle threshold of an actual trial. The go-away idea operates on a just-in-case basis. "Like a hedge against a jury verdict," the lawyer told me: no matter how airtight the defense's proof, no jury's ruling can ever be predicted with utter confidence.

My insurance company put the Zilkes' go-away figure at $20,000. That way they (and I) would avoid the "crap-shoot" of a trial.

"Wait," I said, "*what?*" How does a case go from airtight to crapshoot? The lawyer said, Well, you know.

In front of twelve angry peers, a crying mother some-times can turn opinion against any defendant. (I sometimes wondered if it was the gaucheness of the amount—why $20,000?—that had activated the Zilkes. I wish I could have asked them.)

It was only when they'd been offered this figure that the Zilkes—maybe wondering if they could get more—had hired a lawyer of their own. And, of course, their new law-yer had said: Yes, you're looking at capital-M millions. (It had been Mrs. Zilke who'd hired the attorney to go after me for a fortune. At least, this is what I got from Mr. Zilke as we'd exchanged a few uptight words at one of the deposi-tions. His offering me that information felt, in effect, like another glass of iced tea.)

And so they had arrived at their decision to sue. And according to my lawyer, to open the possibility that they could impoverish me forever by winning a larger sum than what my insurance policy would cover. I told myself that they had done it without my silly ambivalence. If they were successful, they would ruin the life of the kid they'd prom-ised never to blame, never to target.

Almost exactly five years after the accident, I was visiting my parents when my insurance lawyer called. "Check into a hotel," he told me. "Have your friend David check into a hotel, too. Did anyone brief you from my office why I'm calling?"

"No," I said. "*Brief* me? Wait, is something big happening?" All the fears that were always whispering in the back of my mind rushed screaming to the front. Look right, Look left.

"Okay, I think in the next few hours you're going to be served with a summons," the lawyer said. "But this way, they can't."

I didn't understand the legal maneuverings, the reason for a summons in a civil trial (and still don't). But it didn't really matter what I understood: We were going to court immediately.

Couldn't they just call it off, though? My appearing on the stand, the mother crying and accusing and hating me to my face, all that?

"I hear you," the lawyer said. "*But.* And hey, we're paying for the hotel. No, I don't think we can stop it. We *want* to go to trial. It's a pretty definite win. Their attorney's a jerk, besides. We won't even need to give them go-away money. Take a night. We have eyewitnesses, the cops. At trial, the evidence is with us. And when you have all *that*."

I learned that even indoors, even on a cool night, one could sweat so much that a phone can go slick in one's grip. It was hard not to imagine Mrs. Zilke on the stand, storms crossing her face. And then, on seeing me, her eyes would show the release, the godsend, that blame can be. I asked the lawyer to please not make me go through with it. I could feel the word *trial* echoing in my stomach.

"These things take on a momentum," the lawyer was saying. "Look, how's there any meeting anybody halfway with this? The family wants the millions they want, we're not budging above twenty thousand, which leaves a lot of ground in between. Take a night. Have room service."

I took that to mean I would be going on the stand.

I couldn't stop picturing Mrs. Zilke: her face going cold at the sight of me, puzzled by the obstinate fact of my continuing existence. And every time she would lift her eyes to stare me down, she'd see the person who'd survived her daughter in the one contest that made possible any other.

"We're flexible," the lawyer said, "but we aren't *that* flexible, where we won't fight if we can save this much money. So."

That, I was sure, settled it. The moment felt so decisive: stirring, certain, a thunderbolt. I laid out plans to go to a hotel.

The top, social level of who I was shrank from trial

possibilities. Still, there were deeper, muckier layers. These parts of me didn't mind confrontation; these parts of me felt relief that it would at least now be over. My innocence (or my guilt) would have the official stamp of the U.S. court system. Again, I was mostly terrified. But something in me—the same tiny something that had longed for Melanie Urquhart's anger—craved, finally, a decision from twelve people. They'd hear witnesses, cops, statistics, the journal entry. It would no longer be just my daily fluctuating opinion. The official world would have to listen, nod, and answer the question of that highway and that day. A government-sanctioned conclusion: you are culpable; you are blameless. This could bring ruin as easily as release. But the one sure thing it would bring was an end.

And yet.

With what seemed a shiver of disgust, the proceedings came to an immediate close.

Just hours before the trial was to begin, the Zilkes' lawyer suddenly advised his clients to take the go-away money, the original $20,000. (Minus his thirty-percent cut.) *He* didn't want to go to trial. And, like that, it was over. This is the missed beat at the heart of the story.

For years, as I continued to feel sorry for the Zilkes, I could measure time by calculating how much money they might have earned if they'd tucked away the original twenty grand with interest in some bank.

After everyone had dusted themselves off, had shaken hands and shut off the lights, after taxes, after *years,* the Zilkes by my calculations got something like $9,800 for what had happened to Celine and to me.

All because, as the Zilkes' lawyer finally told them, there really was no case.

Some years ago, researchers at George Washington University studied the psychological effect of what police call "dart-out" deaths and what insurers call a "no-fault fatality": car crashes, like Celine's and mine, where someone hurries into an automobile. In the United States, some two thousand drivers a year survive "dart-outs." And these drivers are more likely to get laid out by post-traumatic stress syndrome than are those who are *irrefutably to blame* in fatal accidents. No one knows why. Probably the brain prefers a sturdy error to fixate on. It's hard to learn so viscerally that the questions of guilt and worth are managed with indifference, by nasty chance.

We'd had the accident at the age when your identity is pretty much up for grabs. Before it, I hadn't been so introspective; I'd had nothing to introspect about. Nor had I hidden anything from the world.

For years, when I woke each morning, no matter where I was—home, my dorm, some friend's couch, a woman's bed—if I took an inventory of all that was good and bad in my life, the good would change (as it tends to do). But the bad remained a constant—Celine's unresolved death, the sharp menace of a trial: that clock that ticked in my life. However, the world now meant to put Celine behind me. The New York Justice System's gaze had moved to newer, bigger problems. No one would *ever* weigh in. I couldn't call a trial for myself, say: "Please investigate me." And so now, forever, I'd need to be satisfied with a personal answer, the one I'd never been prepared to give myself.

I thought my trial's collapse would bring—to use a dicey, odious buzzword—"closure." But there was no end to something like this, of course. For me the question, the black scribble in the margin, will always be Celine.

The biggest fact about me—the part that threw me into three dimensions—was her. My accident explained frowns and, for better or worse, gave depth and chiaroscuro to smiles. It revealed everything about the personality I'd created for myself, starting from age eighteen. But it was not something you say to people. I was less fully developed than the chimps in that Amy Hempel story. I didn't have access to a language of grief.

So: hiding. For example, on dates when I traveled the city as a single man. Every new person you date is a freshly arrived celebrity on your radar: you have to learn her backstory, how she ended up on the studio lot, what roles she can play, if she's funny, charming, angry, sensitive. At the restaurant or wherever, I'd be talking, just getting-to-know-you stuff. But I'd have to also wonder: When do I tell her? *Can* I tell her? The answers were nearly always "Never" and "No."

I did spill the story to a few women—often those who, judging by their own hesitations, seemed to have scraped through some trouble of their own. Women who'd faced something ambiguous or complex in their parents' lives (we were that type of cohort). This came up a lot, small winces around the topic. Or maybe they'd had some wounding challenge (anorexia, depression, romances gone sadistic) during adolescence. I felt pulled by the lure of hard-won wisdom.

And so I would find myself confessing to women out of some dull and indefinable obligation, as someone else might feel about a schizophrenic family member or a stint at juvie. You think you know who I am? Well, here's the guy very much behind the social Darin.

But then, I hated the reaction. They grew tender—they patted, deferred, nuzzled. They *forgave*. I saw them really begin to watch me. I felt the web of moments they cleared from certain interactions, that they wiped off the face of a conversation: Ah, he's like this because of *that*. There was something gross about it. Even the truth had a lie's sourness. This was the big problem of confessing, the problem of recognition. I had to do a mental squint just to see myself. And rather than turning life more difficult, as I thought it should, the declaration always got me to feel I'd used Celine's death to obtain softer hours, gentler treatment.

There had been one young woman who'd come out of a long and life-threatening sickness. When I'd owned up to her (I thought: This woman's life has been so difficult, but now she's in the clear. She *must* have the right thing to say), she simply, cheerfully, and forthrightly stepped out of the momentum of our relationship. What she now wanted from her newly healthy life couldn't be guaranteed by me: a lucky passage, an easy, bright course. I understood. Whenever I visualize this non-relationship, I see myself grounded at a restaurant table (I told her in a gloomy bistro) and then her naturally migrating to a better, more livable climate. Her manner was a combination of supportive and *adios*. This seemed just. It seemed self-protective and—considering the eighty-odd years we're given to find our best accommodations on the planet—right.

Nevertheless, with others I acted it all out anyway, falling into my scripted role of assisted suppliant. And felt disgusted—with the unannounced caresses, with myself for accepting them. For allowing myself to be pressed further into an artificial role. "Aw, everything's okay," said a huggy med student. Her name was Cindy, and her hands were ineffectual balms: poking bones, cold fingertips on my cheek. "Oh, sweetie honey," said Felicia, a not-quite-love-match sitting on her studio apartment's lumpy futon. A TV was glaring across the small dinner table. She reached for the remote, and whatever show had been on now lowered its voice, and I saw Mr. Zilke putting that coaster underneath my iced tea. (TV seemed, to Felicia, inappropriate background for the discussion.) No matter how stark the trauma, life—wet rings on wood, television's surges and volume drops—kept on. "That's got to be one of the saddest things I personally have ever heard," Felicia said. "But you have *me* now." She often listened to The Cure and was in thwarted, tragic love all the time. And here's Stacey, who was acting like Juliette Binoche in *The English Patient* (the movie we'd just seen): "I'll take care of you."

"Um, I don't know," I said—and said. I kept waiting to become more who I thought I should be. Sometimes I would think, appallingly: "Good." Or, if I was in an optimistic mood, I hoped the woman might actually tell me something that perched in the soul and sang the tune.

Instead, Stacey's eyes got big and wifey. Felicia just scooted closer.

"It's been easier than I thought," I'd say drably, if I wanted to look brave. "I don't know."

"I'm sure it can seem easier, might be the way you feel sometimes," Felicia said. "*But*."

"Thank you, though," I'd hear someone with my voice say. "You're very kind."

(It was like this with everyone but the newly healthy girl at that gloomy bistro—Jacqueline. When I told Jacqueline, she slitted her eyes. She was making wind-resistance and weather calculations, anyone could see it. She already had the elsewhere stare of a break-up. I dropped a clumsy hand to the table and splashed my salad. Then, months later, I ran into Jacqueline again. I was now taking classes in an MFA program. At a party thrown by a student I knew, there was her trademark glossy dark hair and the flash of her teeth. Jacqueline really stood out amid the frayed ends and premature grays of grad school. I asked if she'd ended things because of what I'd told her. And she said—this was so diplomatic, it became one of those details I made a point of remembering, in case I'd ever need to reproduce it—"You just seemed like you had a lot to work out, Darin. And I thought maybe you could work it out easier without having to worry about how you sound to someone else."

"I don't," I told her, "blame you"—and realized I was quoting the Zilkes. I wondered if that was why I'd asked her: to have their words in my own mouth. The words, however, were untrue. I identified with Jacqueline—I wanted an easy life, as well—and stood watching her sullenly with clipped, cloudy wings. But I did blame her. And the words tasted unclean in my mouth.)

It's as if there's some pheromone of tact and sanctity given off by people whose suffering embarrasses others. Most of these women understood how and why I was behaving the way I did, before I had even behaved. And their sense of me, I realized, was dull and limited, but essentially accurate. (I'm not proud to admit that I found a way to shed the chafing habit of unwarranted sainthood: I broke up with these women.) Anyway, you see why I told so few people, and so rarely. It always ran conversation into the sand.

But I did have a somewhat normal and fun middle-twenties, or at least a multifaceted middle-twenties. And things had been happening in the world that anyone my age had to be at least faintly aware of: the United States had asked Iraq to step outside, then a Democrat came to occupy the White House for the first time since I was nine.

Mostly, I was trying to move on. Even though my thoughts did tend, still, to slip inward, to the incident that was the reference point for every sorrow that came my way. ("Happiness is the greatest hiding place for despair," Kierkegaard once whimpered.) And I was very mindful that Celine didn't have a fun or normal middle-twenties, or any middle-twenties at all.

When I was twenty-six, I somehow ended up on a first date at the movie *I Know What You Did Last Summer*. Which has at its crux a moment in which a teenager hits someone with his car. My breath went pinched.

I thought I was no longer the terrified kid who couldn't think without visualizing Celine, who couldn't visualize Celine without shaking. I thought the past could no longer vaporize my day-to-day life. But now I was having an animal response: I couldn't watch.

"We have to get out of here," I said. "Please." This was about thirty minutes into the movie.

My date didn't want to leave at first. I'd only just met her. But she'd seemed witty and spirited (if very pale), having crossed the lobby with her Christmas-ribbon smile and her good job in publishing. Now we slunk out of the theater.

Or, we were trying to: we had to stand up, block the screen for people who'd merely wanted a good scare. I was obstructing the fantasy with the real thing, though only I could understand that.

Once we got clear of the cineplex, I told her everything. The response was a stunner, out there on the sidewalk—a gruff note of grievance. Maybe I was mishearing; maybe this was her way of warming up toward being sweet and caressive.

"Christ, Darin, don't you think of *her* sometimes?"

She shook her head, even though she was still smiling a bit. She whistled through her teeth. *"Fuck."*

I turned out to be perfectly, officially wrong. This wasn't caressive. This was pissed.

"It's so goddamned selfish for you to feel bad for yourself," she said, a hand at her pale forehead. "I'm not being rude."

Wait a second, here. Of course I think of Celine sometimes.

"Yeah well, fine. But do you think about her *enough*?"

Celine's eyes getting teary after she tripped stealing third base in little league; Celine crackling over pebbles on roller-skates. Celine not being able to stay awake to the end of *The Wizard of Oz* as a kid. Her father (as Celine got dressed for her first date) singing a goofy, made-up song from her infancy. Sixth-grade Celine getting sick to her stomach on doctor's-office candy after a flu shot. These brain montages were how I saw her—and often still see her. Aches and TV shows, family memories. Other times I construct the life she would've gone on to have: Celine wearing a long good coat, in her kitchen, flipping through envelopes to find a med-school acceptance letter. (This is a patently middle-class swirl of images, but I can't deny who I am; I can't unsee what I see. My pictures of a happy life are, intractably, those of ambition cultivated and rewarded.) Sometimes this story line includes rash, dangerous romances, nice solid domestic contentment, shattering health problems: everything, anything but nonexistence.

Or actually, everything and anything but the real Celine. My date, in her way, had been right. My mind was unrelentingly narrative: I imagined the loss of possibility, of chapters, scenes, minutes, of events and kisses and steam escaping the radiator behind Celine and her husband's bed, with their kids in another room. I could feel what I felt about the loss of that. I even allowed myself to imagine her father. Alone at the kitchen table, lights off, not a voice in the house, passing a bottle of something square, bracing, and amber from hand to hand: a movie cliché flickering within the perimeters of recognizable devastation. But I was never brave enough to picture the one thing I knew to be true—Celine lying in the grass on the median strip, her eyes staring only a couple inches above her face, the last bit of time she ever saw.

"It's okay that you called Mr. Zilke a prince, Dad," I had ended up telling my father that morning of my first hearing.

"I just didn't know how to react," Dad had said. "Because even with the lawsuit and the suing for millions and, let's be frank, a broken promise, I still empathize a lot with their family."

"How much thinking about it would be enough?" I was saying to the date now, in front of the cineplex. "What's the amount you're looking for?"

"Ok*ay,*" the date said, and laughed.

She had a cheerful, almost childish voice—a voice I'd come to hear often in publishing meetings, a first-day-of-schoolish excitement and forthrightness. New subjects, new students every semester.

"How can you even go on living?" said the date.

Whoa. I buckled a little and went: "Um."

And like that, Celine was here too, right with me the way her mother had wanted. She was saying: *Yeah, I want to hear the answer to this.*

Anyway, pretty quick, in my mind, I got really sharp: unruffled in James Bond tux, letting drop an epic retort while laying down *beaucoup* eight balls at the baccarat table on some island somewhere. I put up my mental dukes; I was all ready to give the date my best.

"I don't know. I just, well." And then I coughed up: "Uh"—a kind of vocal grimace.

"Yeah," she said in her wronged voice, "that's what I thought." Who was this person with her Kleenex skin and her internship and that smile and did she kick puppies for fun?

"You have no idea how much I *have* thought about it," I said, prim and soggy.

"And so you think, what, Oh, why did this happen to poor me? Why can't I go to a movie all these years later? Hark unto this sad story about *me*."

Her crossed arms told me that the conversation was over. But there was a cold playfulness to her face, the kind you'd see in a kid who has just gulped down, in front of a hungry sibling, the last cupcake at the party. I stood under the theater's electric red tickertape, movies going around over my head like a thought bubble: I KNOW WHAT YOU DID . . . THE DEVIL'S ADVOCATE . . . MOST WANTED . . . EVENT HORIZON . . . A LIFE LESS ORDINARY . . . THE ICE STORM . . . I KNOW WHAT YOU DID . . .

I probably looked tearfree and sturdy, and I finally left for the subway without walking her home. "Okay, then," is all I said to her, more preset civility than real goodbye. And the question I'd asked myself right after the accident had yet to be answered, after eight years: *Would I ever get over this?* (I know how this must read—my being focused on my own emotions right as she accused me of being self-absorbed—and I don't defend it.)

A little later on, the date phoned me. She'd often thought of committing suicide in high school by swerving into oncoming cars, she said. This call was meant to be her apology.

"I came close a few times, usually when it was late," she told me. "You know, headlights coming my way and I'm really depressed, nights like that."

Martin Amis has written that we all hope, modestly enough, to get through life without being murdered. A lot more confidently, we hope to get through life without murdering anybody ourselves.

"All right," I said to my date, just as I was hanging up the phone, because what else was there? I pictured a bicyclist on the edge of vision: the dark speck of Celine. "All right, then," I said. "All right."

4

"My ideas, my language, support me in the face
of disastrous horror over and over."
                                        —Harold Brodkey

"I see here you went to Tufts," a prospective employer would say.

"English major," I'd tell the guy. "Concentration on creative writing." (But would I get fired if this person finds out what I've done?)

"We cover the financial-technology beat," the guy would say—turning over my scant resume, his face dimmed by boredom. "Nothing creative about the writing *here,* young man, I can tell you that." He'd lean forward. "Can you go really, really non-creative?"

"I'll ignore my finer instincts." (But so, am I being ambitious enough for two lives? Is this a good enough job?)

As I moved into my late twenties, as I got to the bridge that would carry me to the thirties and beyond, I realized I'd absorbed Celine's mother's request. When I thought about her now, it was about trying to live well enough for two, *successfully* enough—with enough diversions, enough achievements—for us both. And Celine herself started coming with me, on job interviews, dates, everywhere. I thought of her each time I drove by a bicyclist. (Which happens a lot more often than you think. I'm guessing that's not something most drivers register.)

Mrs. Zilke's extracted promise felt immutable. Each equivocation and hedge, every dawdle; each dereliction and misdemeanor—all the human stuff of growing up—seemed to count against me on some celestial checklist. I'd later think of Celine at my wedding and when my wife told me that she was pregnant. Name an experience: it's a good bet I've thought of Celine while experiencing it.

When I was twenty-eight, my hair went gray and I had stomach surgery. I'd been grinding out my insides. The squinch, the clench, had followed me from freshman year of college on. I was almost six-two and weighed a hundred and fifty-eight pounds. There's only a certain amount of acid you can create before it starts consuming everything. I was eating myself from the inside.

New York's best stomach surgeons—the surgeons you would want to cut you open, if such a cutting were called for—didn't take insurance. So I had to settle. I needed a procedure called a *Nissen fundoplication*. This marries a fairly caveman straightforwardness to NASA-grade sophistication: a doctor manipulates two laparoscopic robot hands to tie your stomach around your gullet and stick it there. (When the tummy is pinned in the shape of a folded-up change purse, acid can't spew back up the esophagus.) I had the surgery in 1998 at the one shitty local hospital that would take my shitty insurance, the Cabrini Medical Center.

Heading to one of Cabrini's surgery theaters, I'd gotten stuck in a bizarre traffic jam; different hospital people wheeled me and two patients I'd never seen before to a bottleneck point (stretchered, gowned, at one of the obvious precipices of a life), and they simply left us there. Our gurneys lined up side-by-side, in a kind of vestibule. The scene felt ghostly and almost comic, a small-scale First Circle. I hadn't eaten in twelve hours and, in my condition, every swallow came like an act of courage. We patients all raised our heads to look at one another—three men made of bedside promises, of cold feet, of life lurch. I was the youngest by fifty years. We each kept totally quiet, very somber. I remember the room as eye-stingingly bright. The other patients showed the frog spots and lack of vehemence that men often have in the last panels of their lives. The hospital went bankrupt pretty soon after this.

I don't want to valorize anything. I don't want to make this more than it was. No false drama: my stomach hurt, and then it didn't. The Nissen fundoplication worked. I thought I'd been fixed for good, but this turned out to be not so. A few years later, I'd lost weight again. I found myself under that haze of mystery discomforts called IBS. It was pretty rough. And as soon as I had handled *that,* I suffered another murky ailment called CPPS (chronic pelvic pain syndrome). My internal climate was a hurricane alley. Emotions blew through, downing power lines, hefting cars onto roofs, destroying the finish. Low trees, dead wood thrown across traffic. That's the force of guilt for you.

During the worst of this I was essentially alone. Then I met my wife.

"I want to tell you something," I said to her, to the woman I'd ultimately marry.

"Tell me what?" Susannah said. This was several weeks into our romance. It must have been about a year after my stomach operation. I was standing at the farthest edge of the twenties, and the sad, steel-gray bridge I mentioned—the thirties and beyond—it wasn't so bad once you looked at it. I was getting to know that most things, as you approached them, were like that. The scary thing about drawing near milestones was merely that you weren't there yet. Once you arrived, they turned familiar—you were in the landscape. They could be dealt with.

Susannah said: "Something bad?" and I scooched around to find the carefree side of my chair.

I tried not to feel the two poles: the excitement of saying something that was sure to be a gongish way to get her attention, and the desire for it to be a less-than-cataclysmic admission. Every time it became social, it felt like a lie. So I tried to say it without having any emotions at all. Any emotion amounted to my playing a part, instead of simply *being* the part.

"Yeah," I told Susannah. "It is a pretty bad thing I have to tell you."

In some ways I remained like the guest arriving at a dinner party with an expensive wine bottle whose price tag has been left conspicuously unremoved. The me who still wanted the world to notice how upsetting this whole thing was, this core thing, pushed to the front of the line.[3] "It is pretty bad," I said.

It's probably a testament to how Susannah took the news that I can't actually remember what she said. It's nice to think your spouse is better at emotions than you are: it's a reminder of why you made the marriage. She probably didn't say anything. She probably just nodded and let me talk. What I can picture is her look. The rational eyes, the quiet crimp to the brow, the sympathy flaming her cheek. It was this that decided me, that had me feeling normal and in love. I remember that her face just opened. I don't know how else to describe it.

There are some people who seem tickled to take on your sad history as their own. It's an object to cuddle and sculpt to their floating aspirations. They see a chance, in you, to be their best selves. You can be the prettying gleam they turn their profile toward. Susannah wasn't like that. She

---

3. To be fair to myself: I didn't ever tell my story in a wheedling voice. I didn't pursue sympathy as if I thought it was somehow the right payment for any psychic wounds suffered. I didn't throw my sadness around. Most of all, I always remained awake to the only certainty there was: I am here and she is not.

didn't fall into the easy and false posture: "Because you have brought me this problem, I am the expert, and it'll be my opinion and solution you shall treasure."

Susannah shook her head at moments of the story and at others just chewed the side of her own mouth affirmingly. I looked down a few times, when I came to parts about which I wasn't sure I was expressing or even feeling honestly. And every time I turned back, her you're-doing-great eyes were still on me. She may as well have had her hand over mine.

She said something like, "It must be with you all the time, even now"—you know, something unimprovable. (Susannah is not a woman to drag her feet in platitudes.)

Because this was stress-free, I could follow my thoughts on their own steady glide, without hope or push.

"Yeah," I said. "It's pretty terrible."

"I'm sure. But you seem okay, too."

Almost overwhelmingly decent, levelheaded, very stubborn, Susannah's a bit unpracticed at hardship. This leads to a defiantly virtuous optimism. It's tough to be swamped with misery when you're next to a person like that.

"Thanks," I said. "I don't know."

I'm surprising myself by grinning now, just recalling this. There's a pleasant, weird vibe you get from remembering a moment of early closeness with someone, in the time before you realized this closeness was going to become your life. And here again is where a split comes. I smile at that thought; I get to learn how that feels. Celine doesn't. And I remember that she will never get to.

"I can't even really imagine," Susannah was saying. "And it'd probably be distasteful to pretend to try."

She's a tall perfectionist who looks like a soft-boned sister to the Faye Dunaway of *Chinatown*. The same high, regal forehead; tepid blond hair that wrongly gets called brown. She's both striking and practical, somehow, like the string of rope lights around the banister that dangles and loops and steers you upstairs to a nighttime party.

This was probably date number five for us, and already I knew she made sense for me. It's a question of rhythm: walking rhythm, thinking rhythm. Her mental pace seemed sensibly like my own. I'd look over, and she'd arrive wherever I was in a conversation, right next to me. And so I'd been measuring with dread how close we seemed to be getting, because if she *did* make sense, then I would have to tell her, and that would maybe end it all.

"Really," I said now. "Thank you."

"Of course—of course."

Then we just went on with our relationship. Another bridge: going from not telling someone to having told her, to having that moment behind me. Until now, in every relationship, it had always been ahead of me. And then the relationship would vanish. Now was the first time I'd ever seen the other side of the bridge, and there was a person beside me.

"Hey, Darin," people said. They slapped me on the back, they shook my hand with both of theirs. "You made it— you came." I said, "Yeah." I said, "Yup." These were people I hadn't seen since that pre-graduation speech. People who had watched the back of my eighteen-year-old head, watched my lurch for the exit.

Most everyone standing near me now had been balded by time, or at least a little gunked up in other ways—lumps, chins. But we were all doing a lot of generous ignoring. Here were people we had spent our childhoods with. They could not be replaced. North Shore High School, class of '88, was sucking in its gut and stepping into a party. This was the denialathon that is a ten-year reunion: the bad luck and scraped knuckles of a decade gone by.

People who haven't stood together for a long while greet one another in format, in banality. Everyone at the reunion was going out all at once into torrents of cliché—"I can't believe it. Ten whole years! Amazing!"—into gusts of the same old stuff. "Look at you—exactly the same. Sophomore year, buddy. A decade! Man, you look . . . great?"

But everything for me seemed charged, sharpened; every conversation that never departed the shores of "Awesome" and "Good times, buddy—good times" was a relief.

It had taken me days to prepare, and the night before the reunion had been all choked stomach and thoughts that no one would be upset if I didn't show because I hadn't promised anybody. I went because I hadn't wanted to go: it was the strongest, best reason *to* go. And because Celine wouldn't get to attend hers, and we were in this together. Also, the part that hated being tied to Celine (the part thrilled by the collapse of the court proceedings, the part that read response-time library books and memorized a sentence from Celine's journal, something she would never have wanted a boy in her high school to see)—*that* part needed to know if, after thirteen years of side-by-side desks and water fountains and time on the school lawn, these people thought of me as just some guy whose car killed a girl in the final bend of the school year.

Yes—another self-involved question. But a tragedy turns a life into an endless publicity tour, a string of appearances where you actually think in words like "tragedy." I must admit that my having showed at Celine's funeral and at her parents' house had been in some measure marketing decisions. This endless focus group, trying to get my Q rating high enough, all to prove that I was acceptable.

There was also a little magical thinking at work here. I'd been able to convince myself lately that I'd begun "moving on." If I'd paid a price for my role in Celine's death, I'd paid with the wooden nickels of self-pity (in high school) and the rubber checks of denial (until this moment). So I showed up here thinking that maybe I could retype my high-school life entirely. As if one nostalgic evening could give my puberty an ending without drama, a calamity-free changeover to college: as if I could turn my memories into something like yours.

I walked through the murmur of reunion; it was like passing a long reel or frieze of hugging. Everywhere I turned, someone's elbow was poking out from around someone else's shoulder, a woman's hair was bunched over a guy's forearm. Women had taken one another's hands by the fingers and just *looked*. (Women were so much better, still, at touching each other than men.) Ex-bullies chatted up their ex-targets. The jokes and grudges, the gossip and the forgotten social calamities: all these phantoms—in the face of time and change—simply dissipated for most people. At this last realization, my cringing nerves almost stopped me short and sent me home.

It seemed for me, and just me, that high school was still fresh: that a few minutes were in a *Groundhog Day* loop, were endlessly happening. That I even had the freedom to walk among these people amazed me.

"I've heard about lots of these," a former wrestler (low center of gravity) was telling a former mathlete (elongated head poking above the crowd and somehow into gray equations). "And I'd say this is one of the best examples of high-school reunions I have ever heard about in all the years I have been hearing about them."

"You'd need a bigger sample."

"That makes zero sense whatsoever," the ex-wrestler said. "Because who's missing? Nobody. We were a tight class, is all. Everybody decided to drop what they're doing and fly the flag, show their face. I'm seeing everybody I want to see. That's a beautiful thing."

"I'm only saying we'd need a statistical mean, for comparison."

"Yeah, right on, nobody mean. Just good people you love."

The evening resisted my taking its pulse. There was no way to get an accurate reading.

Up the flowered walkway, tug open the banquet door, enter the hall, and watch people's nostrils stiffen as they catch sight of you. See their eyes double blink as they catch themselves about to give voice to the thoughts they aren't supposed to say. All of this blew fresh life into the memory of my guilt. But how did I expect people to respond to me? I *am* the accident guy, after all. I circled the hall. Not as if I were a participant but a sort of avuncular, freelance referee: uninvolved, just making sure traffic was smooth. But then, wait; everyone was staring at *everyone*. This was just the Reunion Experience. You were seeing if time had cut you a better deal than it had everyone else. That's all anyone was doing. And then everyone felt the helpless human tug toward nostalgia, convincing ourselves that something mattered because all of us had done it together.

Driving here, I'd found my hands and feet making certain decisions—figuring what I could and could not accomplish—before I was even aware of it. I'd taken certain back streets, going out of my way to keep from learning whether the quicker route had retained Celine's vacant stare.

There was a mirrored wall. James Harmon and I stood just nodding at each other in front of it. We'd been pretty chummy back in the old corridors; it made this glass wall a desert's covered tent, a safe spot to rest. We smiled. We each asked how the other was doing. (James's skin had cleared up.) We smiled again. Drops of light twinkled in James's glass. The cracks in old friendships are measured in awkward pauses.

A little later (after catching up with Jim, joking with Eric), I stood in front of the banquet hall's sound system, next to some balding dude. We hung out there without speaking for a while, each not revealing that he didn't know the other's name; instead we just acknowledged that we were mutually experiencing something.

The dude leaned to me. "I hear that people are going to go to a bar that's around the corner, that's supposed to be a fun place."

I showed agreement by raising my eyebrows. "The Clark Tavern," I said. My hands I kept tented in front of my chin.

The dude's baldness seemed to come from powerful thought: the hair slipping down the sides of the head, the brain pushing up on the skull like a fist stretching a balloon.

"I've thought about you sometimes, yo," he said. "You're the one who ran over that girl? This'll sound weird. I'm just talking out loud here. But I worried about you. Everyone was very hard on you."

Really? That wasn't how I remembered it. I remembered what had seemed to be a big wave, and once I'd pushed through it, only flat calm sea, and people wanting to make sure I was floating all right.

"Were they hard on me?" I said.

"I really did, man. I thought about you a lot. Like a, What's this guy going to do with *this,* kind of a thing. I was hoping I'd see you here."

My face was burning. Or not burning, just suddenly huge and gawky. I needed to get this gawky thing away before I bumbled into somebody. So that's what I tried to do now, with this dude: "Okay, then." Nod, handshake, bye.

After that, every conversation was a swerve. I'd see people I recognized, move close, my courage would conk out, so I'd walk past. Their faces would form into a greeting and then congeal a little as I glided by. *Was that Darin . . . ?*

I'd been wrong. Maybe these people could lay sprawled in their own nostalgia. But I couldn't join them. My thoughts kept flying head-first into the pane of glass that kept me outside of everyone else.

"Oh, I don't associate you with *that,*" a woman named Kim told me a few hours later. By now the night was huffing and puffing toward the finish line.

She and I had stepped out onto the lawn. I had always really liked Kim in school, when she'd been the fluent, prim girl dating Jim. Kim had become a smoker—so there was that gentle distress of seeing people from high school practice adult vices without calamity—and it was because she'd headed outside to burn a cigarette that we now stood here in the cold, just beyond the door, where people expelled long, sighing, dry clouds.

"Thanks," I said, "for saying that." I was obliging too much. "Yeah, I remember you from a lot of different years, as well." This was a case of my deliberately misunderstanding: and why? To make her clear it up. To make her say it again. Guilt makes you behave in ways that get you to dislike yourself, that make you go through more guilt.

She fired up another Marlboro Gold: match crack, instant light on lips, her bunched chin. "I mean, people I think know it wasn't your fault."

"Oh."

"—or even think about it when they first see you," she said.

"Well, good." I nodded, only now recognizing the indiscretion of having brought it up.

She waved at the cigarette smoke in front of my face until it was gone.

At my most confident, I blush and my gaze veers. But when feeling unrecognizable, I'll make sure to look you right in the eye.

"Thanks," I said.

The whole wistful mass of us migrated to the Clark Tavern—carpooling in big noisy departures, that zip and lurch of a family van filled with high-schoolers who'd put on years like weight, but who remained their juvenile selves, after all: hooting out windows, greeting and upending the night. It was like rehashing graduation. We'd left a place that was only us, and entered the world's tricky spots, where people didn't know our stories and had to be approached with suspicion.

But hadn't Kim said exactly what I'd wanted her to say? Why had there been no quick-focused humidity around the eyes, no stinging grateful rush? That my ex-classmates didn't think about Celine even when they saw me scattered other ideas in my head. It was as if I knew less than I had when I'd left Manhattan to come back out here.

Inside the bar, everyone kept snapping photos, or they stared at one another, stares of real intensity—drawn out, blatant, ex-friend to ex-friend. They were hoarding new memories, images to last the decade until next reunion.

Kim had gathered some friends, women. We were all leaning forward—in the way of people at bars—straining to hear over music. (Mullet-rock, thudding from nearby speakers.) I was aware of other people's hair very near my face, that warmth. Everyone was nodding.

"And nobody, nobody here anyhow"—Kim drew a little sundial in the air with her finger—"really knew what's-her-name, the girl, since she wasn't in our grade. *Celine.* So anyhow, our sympathies were with you."

And nodding went around the circle again.

Part of reunions is reenacting the whirl of departure over and over. Every few minutes at the bar somebody would make a sloshy toast and then a dramatic exit: hugs, complicated handshakes, punching email addresses into cell phones. We'd become used to one another again and were saying goodbye again.

I don't even know how I'd gotten Kim and her friends discussing the accident. Ten years on, talking about it remained a crackling horror. Probably, just by acting weird, I'd shown myself stained by the blemish of it. Whatever private anxieties we endure are, of course, never really private. Our own dissembling behavior guarantees their eternal, public return.

"Thanks," I said. "But it's just—" And why couldn't I let it drop? All they'd done was agree to try to buck me up. I wanted to shout: *Come on, someone died!*

"Okay!" one of Kim's friends said, clapping once to ring in a change of subject.

The nodding petered out. I was aware of people's hair no longer being near my eyes. And it felt as if the music suddenly got louder again. The moment had lifted its gates from around us.

"Thank you," I said, "all of you."

"Don't sweat it." Kim tilted her thin, savvy face. I never want to talk about this again, her expression said.

The social-approval me—like the smoke that Kim had earlier waved from my face—seemed to just go *poof!*

And now I was the one gushing my way down the bar, handshaking, hugging, giving out my business card, getting it confused with other people's, so that a few times the card I gave out was someone else's and we had to re-exchange. Maybe some friendships had been relit here, but I doubted it. What was said between this group who had been the stars of each other's lives had been said already, or wouldn't ever be said.

The bald dude I'd stood next to in the reunion hall was moping in a corner: hand around a plastic cup, beer slobbering down his knuckles. This guy looked handsome in a diminishing way. Ignore all the scalp and some excess under the chin and he could still have been eighteen. He kept staring at the mirror behind the taps, and that's where our eyes caught.

He raised his nose, a quick and wordless *What's up*. He was one of the people who'd been remembered by no one, and I thought to give him a backslap, learn his name, but that felt false to me, too. We face-gestured at each other a second time. And next (because life isn't any more afraid of cliché than we are) I jostled out the door and saw a good friend of Celine's. This guy had maybe even been her boyfriend: part of Melanie Urquhart's clique.

He was talking close with arrogant lips to some people I had barely known even back when. His hair was neat as a haiku. And everything seemed just as it had with Melanie ten years before. The guy showed me a rigid, squint-eyed nod. I paused, my cheeks went warm; I scuttled off to my car. I hated that moment: I was angry at the pause, angry at my legs. I had neither sauntered right over to say hi (*This is behind me*) nor kept moving with my head up (*You think the wrong thing about me, and it doesn't matter*). Maybe this is as near to time travel as we can know. Not the sort that undoes events, but the situations (the same faces, words, and gestures; the same internal responses) that bring back former selves. Everything between past and present hadn't disappeared but grown incredibly slim, a wall between now and before that seemed to occupy no space at all. I was the person I had been. This guy was who he had been. Someone all of us used to know was long dead. And the person who'd killed her was making his way home, after pointedly not ordering a single alcoholic drink because he didn't want anyone to see him and have DUI thoughts.

Four years later. It was after 1 a.m., the window cracked open. Breeze and quiet. The empty platform of a night, waiting for the next day to roll in.

"What's on your mind?" Susannah was asking.

We'd just moved in together. I'd climbed out of bed, walked to the kitchen.

Susannah said, "How often do you think about it?" She was rubbing her cheeks awake. "So I'm right, aren't I? The car crash."

"Probably less than once a day," I said. "I don't know."

The accident still turned me shy. She came up to face me. I said, "I guess once a week, maybe."

We'd been together a pretty long while, and by now could decipher the intonation of the glance. "I'm just asking," she said.

"That's a lot less than I used to think about it," I said. It was shyness not unlike the feeling you get in classroom dreams about being unprepared for the surprise oral exam. I said, "Why 'just asking'? Do I sound touchy?"

"You still use 'once a day' as a point of reference? How often did you used to think about it?" She moved to the kitchen table. "Not touchy, Darin—it's just, you never bring it up."

Susannah's mix is innocent and hardheaded; she settles on a position without worry, and stays put.

I squinted and grimaced my authentic surprise. "I can't *believe* it's down to once a week now."

A garbage truck blustered past: clang and rattle across a sleeping street.

Relationships are physics. Time transforms things—it has to, because the change from *me* to *we* means clearing away the fortifications you've put up around your old personality. Living with Susannah made me feel as if I had started riding Einstein's famous theoretical bus. Here's my understanding of that difficult idea, nutshelled: if you're riding a magic Greyhound, equipped for light-speed travel, you'll actually live through less time than will any pedestrians whom the bus passes by. So, for a neighbor on the street with a stopwatch, the superfast bus will take two hours to travel from Point A to Point B. But when you're *on* that Greyhound, and looking at the wipe of world out those rhomboidal coachwindows, the same trip will take just twenty-four minutes. Your neighbor, stopwatch under thumb, will have aged eighty-six percent more than you have. It's hard to fathom. But I think it's exactly what adult relationships do to us: on the outside, years pass, lives change. But inside, it's just a day that repeats. You and your partner age at the same clip; it seems no time has gone by. Only when you look up from your relationship—when you step off the bus, feel the ground under your shoes—do you sense the sly, soft absurdity of romance physics. It had been four years since my ten-year reunion. I did math in my head about Celine all the time. I'd struck her bicycle when I was eighteen. I was now thirty-two: closing in on a decade and a half since the accident. I'd entered adulthood sensing Celine with me. I'd entered romantic life sensing Celine with me. The person inside the bus, ignoring the stopwatch that measured years, had my teenage face.

Discussing the accident with Susannah now, I felt the brain-hesitation, the sudden focus you get before a life shifts.

"I think," she said, dropping into a seat at the table, "we need to discuss it."

I sat, too.

Susannah kept talking. Asking did I think of going to a therapist ever—is there something you need that *I* can do? We'd recently ratcheted up our commitment, and this was night-speak, pledged allegiance; it hardly mattered what she said, more that she was taking the time to say it. Really, honey, have you considered therapy, which is something I can help you with.

"Hard to believe that it's down to just once a week now," I repeated. Was the decreased frequency of my thinking about Celine a good thing or a bad thing? "It sounds shitty out of my mouth," I said.

"Not at all," she said, lowering eyelids, talking fast, crumbs of reticence.

Whenever I got tired of—not tired of; self-conscious and immature about—examining my own motivations, an untrusting part of me examined *her* motivations. I could see calculation in Susannah that she was unaware of. (Or could I?) It was in her interest, as well, not to linger at a moment when I questioned my goodness. Maybe it would start up her doubts about me. And nobody wants to go through that.

"Well," she was saying, "it's like what's the name of that term? No, it seems strange you'd want to deal with this by yourself." Her forehead made its crinkles; she crunched her eyebrows together. There was something both fussy and loving in this. "Survivor's guilt. *That's* the term," Susannah said.

She got up and went to the fridge.

"Really, Darin, what about just talking to somebody?" she said. "I mean a new . . . someone."

I waved her off with a gesture that meant *phooey*. She'd heard about my day with the Shrink, that rough, wet afternoon.

"I really question your decision not to try," she said, in a darker voice.

Whoa. I couldn't believe it. Was she going to let me down? Was I going to tell myself she'd let me down, just so I could avoid talking about it?

She lifted her eyebrows, to say that she was looking for some response. My brows frowned out an answer: I have no response, because your idea's unwelcome. It's a totally unwelcome idea. All the New York street noise was getting blown right back in the window.

Susannah turned, and was now reaching and digging something out of the refrigerator.

I crumpled back in my chair distractedly, rudely. "I don't know," I said in a mock-tired voice. "Why would you push this?"

Susannah pretended she hadn't caught my tone. Outside, there was wide 9th Street, the livid brick of Methodist Hospital, then Prospect Park's great isolating meadow. My cheeks started guiltily to burn. Was it really down to just once a week now?

Susannah came away from the fridge holding a pitcher of water. She walked to the counter, poured out two glasses, then handed me one. "Well," she said.

I had waited a long time, knowingly or not, for this moment. Things seemed to be falling away between Susannah and me.

"Well," I said.

This all must read as communicative impotence. But because of my shared perspective with her, and all the couple-impressions we'd logged—all our new knowing—I'd gained a kind of microtonal purchase on hearing that "well" of Susannah's, just as I bet she had on mine. Hers carried two meanings, I thought: *If you choose not to try therapy, I'll still be here for you—but you have to recognize that it isn't your issue alone anymore.* All this felt approximate and submarine, as if we'd both gone deep into the tide of this moment. It was a larger and more complete moment than simply the words that were like whitecaps on the surface of it. All moments are like that. But the rare thing is to have a clear sense of this depth, and to know another person is sensing it, too. Susannah now gave a resolute, palms-up hand gesture that meant, I thought, even more supra-lingual stuff—something about her character, about her manners and doggedness. (The message of *my* "well" was simple: Sorry for having been a jerk a minute ago.)

"When I figure out what I think and feel about all this," I told her, "I'll talk about it with you."

She brought that gesturing palm to my cheek.

"Anyway, I think I'm getting there," I said. Susannah said okay. Her hand slipped from my face. We went back to bed. That was it.

In fiction classes—or in the novelist-as-humble-cobbler image, *writing workshops*—you find that epiphany has a pretty high rate of occurrence. It's a story, it's tidy. At the end, the hero finds himself standing under just the right tree, reaches up without quite meaning to, and plucks down just the right fruit.

But when you tell your own story honestly, that epiphany thing is rare: there is no walk, there is no fated grab. You try every fruit, or forget there even are trees, and wander from forest to forest, losing sight of any destination. The only changes are emergencies or blessings: when you wake up, notice the surroundings, then fall back, and wander more. And if you're lucky you end up walking again through a life where you're never called on to do too much noticing.

So there isn't any single moment I can point to that scored *when I began to feel better*. I think my job here is simply to dredge it all up, to offer a lumpily dutiful telling of my own life. This is what guilt is like, this is what grief is like, this is how a life forms: when you *can't* ignore, when it wraps itself around one event like a vine clutching a rock. Every direction the vine takes will be determined by that stone. The growth is what you see. But if you look farther down, what you find is the rock.

There were times, in the middle of the night, when I'd come awake and wonder which of us would die first. Cold air above the humidity of the bed, Susannah's mouth open and fishily helpless next to mine, and I'd think: *Me*. Maybe this was more than a trick of the mind. Maybe this was Celine. Celine with me, her words hard, posthumous, and clear: You, Darin—*you* are going to die first.

I got through my twenties and early thirties only by rely-
ing on one thought as hard as I could: Celine had committed suicide. She'd committed suicide through me. I was no
more responsible than is the bullet that comes out of the
chamber. Etc.

Without those blinders—and the thought was a blinder;
it allowed me to move her parents, her funeral, what I'd
been thinking about in the car the second before I encountered her body, out of the frame—without those blinders
I wouldn't have made it.

That certainty got me through the first ten years. I nur-
tured the idea, watered it, saw it ripen, stared at it. Wherever I was, I could summon it.

There are different brands of ignorance: the static of
perplexity, the spun silk of denial. People are too hard on
denial. Shrinks have theories to confirm, patients to com-
mand into the breach. But a person has only a problem, a
souvenir, a life to shoulder through. We need to tell ourselves whatever is necessary. I do think real analysis would
have let in unsafe doubts too soon, like unlatching the great
wooden horse and then just standing aside as all the sandals
and swords ambled past.

My talk with Susannah, with its little aha—*Hey, I've started to think about the crash a lot less often than I had been! What does that mean?*—allowed the truth to begin taking on more shape than I could have handled before. Okay, why? It is worth considering why. The accident and its aftermath became not simply mine but part of the relationship. Celine was a way we communicated. What a horrible fate for a ghost. She was absorbed into the thousands of things that were part of us. Once upon a time, this was what I'd wanted to do with those two unfamiliar girls on the median strip, and also in front of my classmates at graduation. I'd gotten Susannah to see the crash as the most dramatic and basic part of me—which it had been, but maybe wasn't any longer. And, certainly, I had tortured myself for feeling nothing special about it (because the official moments of grief handed me not my own emotions, but something fixed and sanctioned, and what I mainly felt was guilt about that). All the same, this awfulness remained part of who I was. And now who I was had become part of who Susannah was. The crash was no longer something that made me half a person.

That's why I went ahead and did it. I finally got my bravery up, I finally looked hard through the window of memory, a neat square cut into the years.

The timing of my decision to write at last about Celine wasn't a fluke. There was a starting gun, composed of two barrels: new fatherhood and the calendar. I was thirty-six when Susannah became pregnant with twin boys. In early 2007, children of my own were on their way, and the accident had happened exactly half my life ago. (And if you lopped off the first few years, because one isn't really quite *there* as an infant, it was more than half my life.)

These are the type of *holy cow*–grade changes that open a new passageway in one's thinking.

I'd written three novels without laying a hand on the subject. I'd talked to interviewers, posed looking silly in magazines. My first book cropped up on bookshelves as I was turning thirty, and I wondered if the Zilkes noticed—if Mrs. Zilke thought it was enough. First novel about twins (one dies, the other can't go on living); second novel about a guy who's a con artist, a fraud, and an impostor all at once; most recent novel about a marriage where the truest thing between the couple never gets spoken. Historical and contemporary, first-person and third-, different fictional stories chiseled from the same real story. But was I pushing myself enough, succeeding enough for Celine and me both, for our two lives?

My moral and aesthetic codes argued against my writing an accident memoir, against my becoming one more person creating an entertainment out of misfortune, distilling honey from vinegar.

"Yes, that's a valid consideration," Susannah said. "On top of which, do you really want to publish something so personal?"

In all this time, I had never heard anything from the Zilkes; the last time I saw either of them had been Mr. Zilke in the courtroom. When I remembered him, it was always as a father offering iced tea and a coaster.

"I just feel like I have to, Sus," I said. And merely having said it brought the buzz of certain decision.

"Okay," Susannah said.

And she kissed me on the cheek—for a beat too long—before leaving the room.

But months passed and I still hadn't made the jump. Instead I published the novel I'd been working on, Susannah and I bought and fixed up a house, we gathered all our stuff and moved in. I was living out a montage of decisions and their upshots—this could have been one of the lives I'd picked for Celine. I took a faculty job at New York University, and Susannah gave birth to our children.

My boys are named Beau and Shepherd and their arrival came like two hard kicks to the chest. Becoming a dad laid open a tender new flank of myself to life's spikier possibilities. My swerve-and-lawsuit past was back—it was shading the way I saw things, like a bit of private weather, or a visor I couldn't take off. What I really kept thinking about: the Zilkes, the nightmare of what they had to live with. Or had the nightmare lifted a bit for them? Couldn't the nightmare please have lifted a bit for them?

One very early morning, alone with my sons, just months into their lives: sleep was a coating I'd been stripped of, leaving my wiring all exposed. Another 3 a.m. had found me holding two babies and two bottles, had me opening another shit-slathered diaper. The typical new-dad distress; the predictable, slapstick wretchedness. But one of my sons now turned to me—and I could tell he was doing so, as it were, for the first time: his look bespoke a little recognition. So I'd been wrong when I'd presumed to lop off the very beginning of a life. We record things right away; what touches us matters. I grasped—with new, gut intensity—that my sons were *mine*. This deep-hitting awareness raked up my different selves. (But couldn't the Zilkes maybe have found a strengthened, cautious love; couldn't I just try, in thinking about who they'd become, to ignore the thorns and likelihoods?) Easing the bottle from Beau's mouth, I could see him—for a half-second, until I stopped myself— as Celine. I had a thought, or at least an upsetting wordless brain throb, about what it might be to make and hold a life and then release it.

"How's the thing going?" Susannah said, against all better judgment.

Whenever I tried even to think how to manage it, the wires would cross and spark.

I was afraid.

"Are you sure you even want to write non-fiction? Or would be able to?" Susannah said one morning, a provocation. One of Susannah's attributes is that sometimes she doesn't know when she's arguing.

Who knows, I thought, perhaps she'd been faking her certainty of my innocence.

So why didn't I just give it up? I had another good reason to. How do you grieve for someone before you start the work of understanding her? It's like trying to worship at the blueprint for an unfinished temple.

Even after all this time, nothing had forced me to examine the accident, or Celine herself; everyone had let me slip through, and I realized the only person who really had the authority to force that examination, for better or worse, was me.

I shouldn't even say I realized this yet; I was only starting to get it. But I knew enough to not give up, when I had given up so often in the past. We contain more than our understanding allows us, at a given moment, to understand.

A September 2009 item in *The New York Times* said that every U.S. death affects, on average, four other people profoundly. Of these affected survivors, something like 15 percent can "barely function." And this decisive suffering— which lasts and lasts, and offers "no redemptive value"—has been given a name, to distinguish it from what used to be called sorrow: *Complicated Grief Disorder*.

Complicated Grief Disorder sounds a lot more potent than what I suffered—though perhaps not so different from what Celine's parents suffered. (It's chronic and intense. It's people deciding that, because their beloveds can no longer walk the streets, they also are unfit to walk the streets. One mother told the *Times:* "Eric couldn't have any more birthdays; why should I?")

The treatment for this affliction is an unprecedentedly rigorous form of the talking cure. And also, maybe, a breakthrough: therapists force patients to relive the details of the death, making them repeat the minutiae of their pain into a tape recorder in front of an analyst. The patient then replays this tape—this doting agony chronicle—at home every day. For months or even years. This would seem, at first glance, like a religious observance or a torture.

But according to the *Times,* the therapy is totemic. It's not about making the tape, or listening to the tape. It's about possession, about having the story in one place. "The goal is to show that grief, like the tape, can be picked up or put away," the article said. In "Treatment of Complicated Grief: A Randomized Controlled Trial," *The Journal of the American Medical Association* declared this tape-and-torment approach "twice as effective" as the conventional therapy used to treat chronic grieving. (Another plus: it also worked much faster.)

In a separate *Times* article, George A. Bonanno, a professor of clinical psychology at Columbia, called the available mourning data "embarrassingly bad" and said "[conventional] therapy for bereavement in general is not very effective."

No one says this new treatment is a complete salve for heartache, nor even that it should be. The *Times* again: "Diagnosing a deeper form of grief, however, is not about taking away anyone's sorrow." "We don't get rid of suffering in our treatment," said one of the doctors. "We just help people come to terms with it more quickly."

Isn't that what we'd all hope—even the dead? That those who have died can lose their hold on the living? That the dead will lose their spell over these poor people.

I hoped to make this book my tape.

"Are you nervous?" Susannah asked, dropping her eyes before looking back at me: a quick shyness that was uncharacteristic.

My 10-and-2 grip on the steering wheel tightened.

"Yeah, a little, I think." My voice sounded surprisingly meek, too.

I fixed my gaze on the windshield. It was ice-crusted; this was in February. I'd been trying to anticipate and then solemnize each brief hill as we climbed it, and all the grassy clearings we passed. This was a strip of road I hadn't seen for more than half a life. I was preparing for the moment when the background—a sheet of stones, trees, lawn, and shoulder—would become the hard foreground, would become the thing that had remade me.

Here I was on West Shore Road, near Bar Beach, where my past had located itself. I was back and, I hoped, changed. A traveler from the world of grown-ups.

Our sons were six months old and fuzzy-headed, and they sat babbling to each other in the back of our Honda. It irrationally frustrated and wounded me that the boys had no idea where we were driving, and I wanted to say— because I know this is true, too—that we were going to the place that had allowed them to be born. I would've been a different person had the accident not happened. Without Celine, I wouldn't have become a writer, I don't think. And therefore I wouldn't have met their mother. I find it an amazing stroke of luck to be married to Susannah. To be a parent with Susannah. That's the meter you come up with, as you approach forty. If your relationship fills you with a sense of luck, you've chosen well. I wanted the boys to know all this, but they couldn't understand it. I don't think even Susannah could understand it as much as I did. The boys kept up their babbling.

Forty minutes earlier, we'd trussed them into their infant seats. The city had thinned and scattered into the placid array of North Shore Long Island. I was driving across that crocodile's back again. Buildings, as if getting the okay sign that the coast was clear, became wider, turned into homes and lawns. Now the talking stopped, and the radio, too. Uphill, downhill, then the road grew bare of towns altogether. It was just a place between places, a place you had to get through, nowhere anyone wanted to be.

"Is this how you pictured it?" I turned my flustered face to Susannah. "Is it?"

There were cars everywhere, people who drove this road every day. The sad thing was not that they had no idea. It was that it wouldn't have mattered to them if they had.

Minutes later I was outside, putting my hand up to oncoming traffic and jogging across the pavement alone. I was moving toward the median strip. Sunlight knifed through a few small areas of snow. My gloves were the kind that have a leather palm-patch to improve the grip. And here I stood, folding my arms for warmth, on crunching grass—the spot where it had happened. Or my approximation of that spot. If Celine lived anywhere, it was here. If the person I'd been before colliding with Celine was anywhere, it was here. February air hurt my cheeks. The breeze felt grainy; there was moisture in it. No crosses or markers set this part of the road off from any other. I looked down; heat from my boots was melting the crust in a small oval around my feet. Which is how insistent a body is, how much energy it has, even when you do nothing.

I spent a long time just looking around. The wind lifted the slender grass shoots every so often, ruffling what seemed like a field of tiny bobbing heads. I stood here taking shallow breaths. I tried not to look over my shoulder at Susannah and the twins. I cleared my mind. I was here again. The February sun, that cold-burning bulb, threw off a faint blue glare. West Shore Road, treeless and homeless, stretched a long way behind, a long way ahead. It must have been the nearby Long Island Sound that put this blue nuance into the air; but I couldn't see the water itself—it was a hunch, a rumor. Maybe Celine's tire had caught on some of the blown sand at the road's edge.

And then I did look into the blue grainy distance, at my family. They waited in the car for me. (But so why had Celine swerved all that way—over *two* lanes, first crossing into one and then, after a wait, into the other?) Maybe she'd been startled by a noise. Or a bee had gone after her hand a couple times. But wasn't there something *I* could have done differently? The only noises now were the muting sound of water someplace else—a whispering repetition—and the gathering and receding swish from an occasional car. These passing cars made our Honda rock a little bit. The two sounds sounded pretty much the same. I was surprised there weren't accidents here every day. What could I possibly have done differently that morning with Celine?

My heart sped up, just as it had a few minutes before, when we'd driven to this place. Whether at any moment she was vivid or faint, forgiving or disagreeable, or nearly gone—Celine had stayed with me. Today's sun was no more than the harsh glower of my past. I saw an office park: big glass Rubik's-Cube buildings across the road, not very far off. There hadn't been an office park here before. The cars on the road were makes that hadn't existed when I'd had the accident. The grass was new, the nineteenth season of new grass. Maybe some of the sand on the shoulder was the same. I felt sad and distracted. Maybe the vaguely respiratory beach and road sounds were the same as they had been. Just sad in a distracted way: that was all I felt. I waved to Susannah and the boys. I don't think they saw me. Or perhaps it was just that I couldn't see them: the windshield was showing the rags and pinks of the sky, and I couldn't make out Susannah's features, only the shape of her head. (I say distracted because the sadness felt docile, and fuzzy.) There was nothing profound about feeling only sad. The car sound on the acoustic asphalt evoked a bit of anti-nostalgia: all the lonely schoolbus waiting of childhood, plus a death. My eyes were dry. I couldn't do what Mrs. Zilke had commanded me to do. If I was able to have just this one life from here on out, what would Celine Zilke do without me now?

I wrote and wrote and listened close for whatever the past was trying to say to me. It was still tough even to think about this girl who died.[4]

I omitted a thousand things, because a life is so much the same thing over and over. I omitted my being a ski bum in Aspen with some friends, including good old frontseat-passenger Dave, and getting so drunk the first night in town that my shoulders went numb; I omitted losing my virginity, or trying and failing to lose it—urging an evening to curl itself away and vanish. Those are what life is, but they are not at all Celine.

Day after day, draft after draft: I was surprised by the stuff that came out—my blunt and jumpy chapter and verse; the brake sounds and disclaimers. Until I started writing this, I'd forgotten the library books, the face I wore in my dorm, the way that Mr. Zilke had been at the court, angry, humble, and sad. And I realized I'd been lying to myself: that fact was the first thing I learned.

---

4. See the way a forgiving brain runs that sentence, even here, even now? *The girl who died.* I still have to fight against being passive, about being shy. Or, if you prefer, cowardly.

Maybe I could have done fifty things to avoid the accident. Left the car in the garage that day. Hurried through a yellow light that I'd stopped at. Gone to the beach instead of mini-golf. Been alone, not talking to friends. But I did all those things, and Celine hadn't done the many things she could have to avoid the accident, either. All the things get done and you regret them and then you accept them because there's nothing else to do. Regret doesn't budge things; it seems crazy that the force of all that human want can't amend a moment, can't even stir a pebble.

"Was it worth the trip out?" Susannah said after a silence, on our drive home from West Shore Road. Everything man-made got taller, shinier—preparing to enter the competition of New York City. "Did it help?"

"Help to write it?" I said. "Or help, generally?"

This was back in the early days in my writing this story. Warmth was surging from the heater onto my face.

Susannah said, "Either one." She turned her head and looked at me. "How do you feel?"

"I don't know." The words, inane and true. "I don't feel—

—much"? "—all that I had expected"? "—something to cap off my experience"?

Part of me was still uncomfortable letting myself feel better about the accident, twenty years after it had happened. I worried what "better" would even mean. The mind is like a fish: stillness makes it afraid.

For a long time I had believed I was missing some crucial and important thing. There was a dead spot in who
I was; a mildew. The same worry for my future that I'd felt
at eighteen, at twenty, at twenty-seven, when that woman
at the cineplex told me there was no way I could live with
such a horrible past.[5]

"So you didn't experience anything too profound when
we stopped," Susannah said. "It's a good sign, don't you
think? Or was it a waste of a trip?"

I agreed it was a good sign.

But often I couldn't do the writing. I'd will myself into
remembering, the way I had tried to will myself to tears
during high school. Ignorance is maybe the most stable
matter there is; it's very hard to lift your personality from
the bedrock of solidified principles, of petrified ideas.

I'd slump there at my writing desk, sweat out six gal-
lons and maybe a hundred words; the next day I'd strain
a little further. And then, finally, on the page, Celine was
there again, cutting in front of me. And I was at the movie
theater with Dave and Jim, not feeling enough and feeling

---

5. I should disclose here: I'd started going to therapy several years before
this—though not (I really don't think) as a response to the accident. I'd gone
with pretty boilerplate stuff: your typical mid-thirties complaints. Trying to
swim *with* the tide of your life's important associations. Squaring ambition
with reality. Just getting one's psychic shit together. My therapist said *how
does this make you feel* and *empowerment* and *a process of healing*. I said, *well, so
you think I'm okay?* She said *patience, patience; that's all the time we have for this
week*. But any knowledge was impossible without my having stared down the
accident. And so my therapy attempts had always been near-misses, fizz-outs
if not outright failures.

so much. And the next writing day, the story got a little more vivid, and the truth more achievable; and also the day after that. It was in the *doing,* the rethinking, the simple inundation of it, like those bereavement tapes on infinite playback in lonely homes.

And at night, I could switch the computer off and walk down the hall to where the people now in my life were making their different sounds.

I don't want to say that in any Proustian sense I'd consecrated my life. You don't create a personal bible by ripping out all the myths.

Here is what I've come up with:

Because I was alive in a certain place, Celine Zilke isn't anymore. That's all this was. Statistics and figures, mathematical anomalies; sour numbers on America's balance sheet. Forty thousand die on U.S. roads every year. (And with almost every fatal accident, someone walks away suspecting he's put on the executioner's hood.) But it was me and it was Celine. She was someone I happened to, someone who happened to me.

I learned to see the accident the way a painter sees a picture—up close, dots of circumstance; step away, an image, stuck and clear. When Celine wrote, "Today I realized that I am going to die," there's a good chance she meant only that she'd come to understand that she would—in the future, when all of us are quietly smudged from the blackboard, one by one—die *someday*.

After I came to accept that, there was just no way not to follow these crumbs of thought to their destination: I can't know—not for sure—if I may have been able to avoid killing Celine Zilke.

We can try our human best at the crucial moment, and it might not be good enough. That I do know.

The girl I killed: never before had I eased up and stood next to those hard words.

The knowledge that shadowed me with its wing—that the only certainty I have is that I did the best I could when she took her inexplicable turn across two lanes—would have painted the younger version of me with guilt. My journal-entry assumptions were meaningless. I'm typing this right now in a library, and there is a calm to my breathing; everything is more or less okay, brainwise. My mind isn't sounding out sharps and alarms: fraudulence, guilt. But I keep spacing, keep looking to Reference, where the lady shushes a hyper young girl, and I begin to cry. I am not weeping, not really. And I think it's from something like relief.

Celine Zilke's life ended in front of me. But I can't access her. I know nothing important, nothing real about Celine except how she died, and that I'm part of the reason she died.

I just read the policeman Paul Vitucci's *Newsday* quote again—for the first time in decades—and it came like a gift from the past. I'd forgotten the completeness of the absolution. It was clear and direct and full enough to seem an express message to this future me, a dispatch meant to comfort and assure.

I remember Officer Vitucci once told me if I'd swerved the car differently that May 1988 morning, I might have flipped it. Say that had happened. Say Celine had lived and I hadn't; what of herself would she need to put to the side, in trying to think about me: the stranger who had managed somehow to swerve *away* from her bike, and who had died because of it?

I used to think I'd like her to not remember me at all. Not to have to contend—at eighteen, at thirty-five, at all life's cozy moments—with a stranger. I'd like her to be spared the feeling that she'd traveled for two decades with a ghost.

But now I don't know. I don't know if that would be fair, or even best for her. And not, I don't think, because I'd want the spirit of who I was to be kept quote unquote alive in her. It's more that if she'd been too comfortable with my dying, she wouldn't have remained a fully live person herself.

It's not that I outran Celine, or that half of my life. It's the reverse. The accident taught me this.

Things don't go away. They become you. There is no end, as T.S. Eliot somewhere says, but addition: the trailing consequence of further days and hours. No freedom from the past, or from the future.

But we keep making our way, as we have to. We're all pretty much able to deal even with the worst that life can fire at us, if we simply admit that it is very difficult. I think that's the whole of the answer. We make our way, and effort and time give us cushion and dignity. And as we age, we're riding higher in the saddle, seeing more terrain.

So it's an epiphany after all. You have it in your hand the whole time.

Whether Celine had been intent on dying that sunny morning or not—this has, in the end, little to do with me. Of course, the new element of doubt effects the wide and somber assurance of those reaction-time numbers I'd needed in college. Suicide is suicide, accident is accident, and ambiguity lives in the gap between. But suddenly—that is to say, after half a life, plus a few rocky months at the keyboard—I finally get it. And it's mountain-stream clear: This tragedy isn't mine to own. It's hers.

What I hated in myself, for more than half a life now, was feeling lucky for being alive. For not being blamed. Merely for being allowed to continue, when Celine wasn't. How could anyone be unhappy about that? But how could a person with my story agree to feel relieved and blessed? The accident has formed me. I can no more discard it than I can discard having grown into adulthood. But I am grown now. And because I am, I can say no. I can say no to the hectoring, blistery hurt. I can say to myself: It's all right to take in the winter beach and grass smells, and crackle back across the sand of the road, and smile at the faces you love.

ACKNOWLEDGMENTS

Every book is collaborative. Or that's what they say. With this book, the truism felt more fully true than it had before. Which is surprising, because what you hold in your hands is an acutely personal story. But *Half a Life* was an out-and-out team effort.

My thanks first to Ira Glass and Jane Feltes at *This American Life* and Michael Rapkin at *GQ*, who edited excerpts of the book skillfully, and with steep compassion. But the thanksgiving doesn't stop there. My wife, Susannah Meadows, and my friend David Lipsky did Lish-grade work on the manuscript. I'm forever grateful.

At McSweeney's, Eli Horowitz was patient and sharp and loving and he improved the book hugely. Dave Eggers was generous, passionate, hands-on—easily the most hands-on editor any writer could ever want. He cared a shocking amount (down to the last disputed semi-colon), and that was very humbling.

I owe Dave and Eli another thanks. They were willing to take a chance on this book as it had been pitched to them; I said I saw *Half a Life* as a forty- or fifty-page oddity. And Eli said, "Whatever it needs to be."

Sarah Chalfant and Scott Moyers at the Wylie Agency—The Amazings—never pressured me to make the book any longer, or anything other than what I wanted to make it. That it ended up coming in at almost four times what I'd planned is a testament to how freely I was allowed to explore.

There were and are also that day's carloads of unfamiliar eyewitnesses, the police officer Paul Vitucci, my friends and passengers David Wohl and Mike and Jeff Newman, my schoolmates Eric Salat and Frank Santoro—and so many people at North Shore High in 1988. My primary mission here has been to make the words of this book an adequate expression of my gratitude.

Finally, my family. If you've read any of what comes before this, you got to see a little of their genius for kindness, for espousal. Bernie and Ellen Strauss, Susannah Meadows, Tracey Hechler—loving advocates, all of them. And finally, Beau and Shepherd, my sons. Thanks for coming.

HALF A LIFE

Darin Strauss

A Reader's Guide

AN ESSAY BY DARIN STRAUSS

By being an author I have in a sense made the
public my confidant.

—Kierkegaard

I

When I started writing *Half a Life,* I thought it would
be an account of one scrubby little terrible accident and
that's all. But the story ended up throwing big shadows.

In 2008, I'd read it (a very short, early draft) on *This
American Life.* A stack of paper, sixteen on-air minutes, the
soft tickle of microphone to mouth. That would, I thought,
be it. Nobody would care too much. I'd been on radio before, and impressed very few. Now I got hundreds of emails,
though—literally hundreds, and immediately.

"[For] the first time in 16 years I now know that I am
not the only human being that knows what this feels like,"
one woman wrote. Another: "My life has changed forever
because I heard it." And one of Celine's friends—someone
I hadn't known—wrote: "I want to thank you for bringing
this memory back in such a meaningful way."

Others asked if I might send them a printout of what I'd read. One of these askers knew a Westchester boy whose car had hit and killed a seven-year-old; another's husband never discussed his sister's death; and another, etc.[1] All these people thought a loved one might be comforted by reading an account of this disaster, of my slouch and bungle against it.

II

In writing, avoid what Saul Bellow called "helpful-to-the-sick clichés or conventional get-well encouragements." That was my exact fear: that I'd end up for sale in the personal-help wing of your local bookseller.

And yet.

There must be a way to confess and avoid confessionalism's dreck. The bullshit of most self-help shouldn't mean that we can't help ourselves by reading, or others by writing.

Maybe this is a peculiarly American idea—that even literature should be pressed into service-industry work? I turned

---

1. Please don't take me as ungracious just because discussing these emails affects my stomach like twelve hours on a trembling airplane. I'd been warned by other novelists turned memoirists, Oh, you'll be overwhelmed, non-fiction's quite different, readers won't respect boundaries, etc. All this turned out to be true. But true in a way that struck me as profound and thrilling, even beautiful. I started up email relationships with a number of readers. But because these relationships are based only on awkward personal revelations, they're delicate. So delicate I'm afraid that, like shadows, they'll die if I shine much light on them here.

for answers, as lit nerds do, to my bookshelf. David Foster Wallace said writing's first obligation is to address what it is to be a human. Or, as has been said about Beckett, of all writers: Literature should give "comfort to those in need."

Like Wallace and Beckett (only quite a lot more imperfectly), I write fiction—that organized, wrought-out thing. So I believe there's not just beauty in fiction's strict form, but also what Martin Amis has called a kind of ethical principle. Fiction writers arrange facts in ways that come to a kind of moral point. Such is the storyteller idea, anyway. But that wouldn't jibe with what I set out to do here— which was? Well, merely to offer up a lumpily dutiful telling of my own life. Anything else would have felt false, disrespectful and false.

But here's a thing I found. Maybe when you loosen a story from the pinching girdles of plot and ironic distance, from rhythm and sophistication—when you take away the casuistry and dazzle of an arranged literary framework— maybe that loss is nearly matched by some gain in simply offering things just (but exactly) as they were.

Besides, when you start really to examine the random pieces of your history, you might start to catch some accents and emphases in the mess. This seemed odd when it happened to me. It was sort of like how, when you stare for a while at one of those books of ocular gimmicks, a discrete image will begin to rise from the page of scribbles.

Those accents and emphases mark out the signposts and mile markers of your own tellable story.

III

Self-protection is a strong instinct, but it has to be overcome when you write down who you are. The drive to self-forgiveness can take you down a pretty distasteful path; there's a lot of kitsch in a brain's sly seduction of itself.

The Complicated Grief Disorder sadness-playback treatment I mention in the book—in fact, the whole glut of post-traumatic stress disorder cures—bundles together a lot of what's in the air, a lot of fashionable concerns, but no morality. The PTSD cure's dutiful enthusiasm about the stems and blooms of depression and guilt may remind cynics of Ludovico's Technique, from *A Clockwork Orange.* (A sadistic criminal is made to watch violent images as he's given an emetic.) Ludovico's works, our dire narrator is cleansed—his ethical will is pulled up by the roots—and we're left in a world of absolution, but no justice.

As I wound down this essay, it just so happened—a correctness that seemed as heartbreaking as it was rigid—that I caught a scene of *Clockwork*'s Alex, his eyes wired open to Ludovico's scrupulous brutalities.

One thing not addressed in most self-help is whether the person *deserves* to get better. Pop psych is no place for ethical quandaries—just the certainty of one's own stainless right to feel good. All I can say about this is: I've tried very hard to avoid any sort of reflexive justification here—to avoid putting my thumb in the scale. That's why I've offered up as many unflattering disclosures as I could remember. (Going to the *movies* the day of the accident, for Christ's sake?) I tried my best to make sure what you hold in your hands isn't just some brief for the defense. Now it's up to you, I guess, to see if I succeeded.

IV

A friend of mine recently had to pull off to the side of his life. His mother fell unexpectedly, deathly ill. He moved to his family home to care for her. He knew this would be very hard. The difficulty, the cost to his mind and heart, topped even what he had braced himself for.

His mother was dying in front of him—in all the physical messiness and gagged intimacies of a drawn-out death. Helping the mother die was exhausting, sad, constant work. And the truth was, she was going to die anyway. My friend learned that it was also true that he could handle this bleak work. And that he owed it to her to handle it. To her, and to himself.

I asked this friend if I could mention him here. His response: "It sounds lame to say that hearing *your* story changed my life but it kind of did. Just knowing someone else has gone through something and made it out. And if you put my story in your book, then maybe some other reader will be affected by *that*. And so my mother's story will be in some small way knitted with that person's story, as well as your story, and my story. And so on."

Morally passionate, passionately moral writing (Wallace again) ideally helps readers feel less alone. That may read as puffed up and kitschy. But it's what I was trying to do here: to be faithful to the memory of Celine, and to all those generous, sharing emails. And so what had started as a personal account of an atypical recovery—basically, of my own fuck-ups and slow learning—has opened for a lot of people into a universal story of how to live with steep grief and unwarranted guilt. And with the running back and forth between shock and anguish—which is shock's finger-pointing offspring. People find their stories easier to live through when they hear other people's stories.

This is how my friend goes about the care of his dying mother: he rises each morning and chops the wood, and carries the water. And he's going to be okay.

A CONVERSATION WITH DARIN STRAUSS

Colum McCann is the author of the novels *Let the Great World Spin, Zoli, Dancer, This Side of Brightness,* and *Songdogs,* as well as two story collections. He won the National Book Award in 2009, has been a finalist for the International IM-PAC Dublin Literary Award, and was the inaugural winner of the Ireland Fund of Monaco Literary Award. A contributor to *The New Yorker, The New York Times Magazine, The Atlantic,* and *The Paris Review,* he teaches in the Hunter College MFA Creative Writing program.

Colum McCann: They say all stories are the same. Of course this can't be true. The poem doesn't swerve and suddenly become a thriller. The playwright doesn't necessarily know how to begin a rhyme. Can you discuss the challenges that face a novelist who switches to memoir?

Darin Strauss: My training and my inclination is to invent. Memoir was in some ways an easier form (you skip the hard, dreaming-stuff-up work) and in some ways more difficult (wait, you can't just dream stuff up?). The novelist has permission to do whatever she chooses to supercharge whatever's interesting in her story. This is also known as freedom. So, had this been a novel, I would've made the court case more steeply dramatic, for example. I couldn't, of course.

But something about the exercise feels, for lack of a better word, pure. Trying only to remember what had happened—but exactly as it happened—and being reverent to the facts: trying to make something artful of that.

The challenge is being true and respectful and stylish, at once.

CM: Which it is. It all comes down to language, the holy word put in the right place. It seems to me that when a writer is working honestly the story finds the right language for itself. It's somewhat mystical. Yet you have to work hard to create the possibility of this happening. And so it seems to me that it's about stamina and desire, listening for the right music.

DS: Exactly: Babel's famous, heart-piercing period. You mention the mystical. I shy from occult descriptions of what we do at the keyboard. But a sense does come—a frizzle that says each book teaches you how to write it. It's different every time, and always requires a mix of inspiration and ass-in-the-chair time. Writing has somehow to involve both a slow patience and a thunderbolt.

CM: This book is full of thunderbolts—wonderful subtle strikes of weather. Everybody is going to want to know if you had ever considered fictionalizing it.

DS: Thanks. But I'd never considered writing it at all. I thought the accident was going to be my lifelong secret, the past I wouldn't let poke into the now. I told almost nobody. Writing began only when we had our twins, when I realized the accident happened half my life ago: impending father-hood tends to focus the mind. I felt with new force that I'd never be able to feel it all—never truly comprehend just how awful the Zilkes' loss must have been. I wrote merely as a way to take hold of my thoughts about this. (I write to figure out how I feel and what I know about something; I imagine you're the same way.) So the book started as a little therapy project, and has ended up with me talking to you here. Which still feels strange to me—the big secret as par-ticipatory event.

CM: Do you think the accident, or your knowledge of the accident, had influenced your fiction in other ways? In the word choice, in the movement of the characters on the page?

DS: Hmm. There is something numinous about writing, something beyond craftsman-y. (We don't discuss this when we teach.) And so I'm wary even now of exploring it. Let's leave a few of the seven veils in place.

CM: You write, "My accident was the deepest part of my life, and the second-deepest was hiding it."

DS: I have a lot of friends who found out about my accident—the death, the lifelong guilt—only through the book, or the excerpts in *GQ* or on *This American Life.* So it was strange; people resented my silence. But I just really wasn't ready to talk about it.

CM: Now you're not only talking about it, but you're making sense of it for others. You're deepening its meaning but also its implications. How much do you consider it to be a project that you wrote for, say, your own children when they get a chance to read it? Does that idea frighten you?

DS: Colum, I don't know how your work intersects your family life. For me, I simply can't wonder how they (my kids, Susannah, my parents, any one particular reader) will respond. That would trip me up at the first word. I may have in mind a Platonic audience: me but smarter, free of prejudice, open, book lovers with a lot of time on their hands, Nabokov's dictionary by their side, etc. And—though I never thought of it before—I guess I see this perfect reader as an adult. (My sons are now three.) All the same, I am anxious for my kids to read this. When do I show it to them? Will it be upsetting? These are the unknowns.

CM: Yes, but they're also the beauties. My guess is that your children will thank you for it. They will say you are a better father for having muscled up to tell the truth.

DS: It's kind of you to say. But my feeling is: I spent eighteen years shrinking from the truth. Sure, I finally knocked at the door of guilt with somewhat decisive knuckles. This strikes me, in itself, as not especially praiseworthy. I don't mean to say it's blameworthy. It's neither one or the other—probably it's midway along the cowardice-bravery continuum. Now, I am proud of how the book turned out; but I've gotten too much public credit just for the attempt. All the same, I do feel lucky that when I knocked, the door opened.

CM: How did your having written about it—this therapy project of yours—change the way you thought about the accident?

DS: You know, Mailer wrote *The Armies of the Night* as a response to an article in *Time.* He thought the reporter had misrepresented his (Mailer's) behavior during an anti-Vietnam march. So Mailer begins his *Armies* by reprinting the entire *Time* article, and then there's this: "Now we may leave *Time* to find out what happened." The resultant book is a four-hundred-page letter to the editor.

I found myself with the same frustration, the same impulse, raised to a higher power. How crassly my local newspaper had portrayed the accident! As if the sadness quotient depended on Celine's having been the most popular kid, the class pretty girl, some kind of prom superstar. I felt protective of the real her, who had been made 2-D by the reporter, simplified into something she wasn't. In fact, maybe that's where my fiction training came into play—knowing how to return nuance to the story, and chiaroscuro. At least, I hope it did. I left the pages of *Newsday* to write what really happened.

CM: Can you talk about the relation between the earlier works of fiction and this book? Similarities of voice, or perspective? Despite that this is a memoir and that those are novels, you wrote them all. They're all Darin Strauss books. Can you find commonalities in them all?

DS: Saul Bellow once said he didn't want ever to go to therapy, because he didn't care to learn why he wrote what he did. Well, I've learned why I have. At the funeral home, Celine's mother told me: "you are living . . . for two people." My first book, *Chang and Eng,* was about conjoined twins—two men sharing one life. The first line is: "This is the end I have feared since we were a child." The narrator's both singular and plural— "we feared . . . I was." Eng Bunker lived as two people and one person.

The Real McCoy centered on a man who threw off his identity, and in coming to New York lived as an impostor. That was how I felt, having fled to the city, having told no one about my past, about who I was.

More Than It Hurts You is about a Long Island family with a terrible secret. . . .

It's embarrassing how obviously I was writing about this incident—without my having known it.

CM: And so now, having written it head-on, what's the difference between examining the accident obliquely and actually facing it head-on, page-on?

DS: One difference is: writing such non-fiction is basically a very public therapy session. As you know, you write a novel, interviewers ask about book-related points of interest. "How'd you come up with that character? What were you thinking with that plot twist?," etc. But when you write a memoir, people ask about your state of mind. "Did writing the book help you? And how do you feel now?" It's a very odd difference.

CM: All right, then. So, how do you feel? I know how I felt when I first read the piece in *GQ*. It took my breath away. Quite literally. I remember gasping a moment. There is so much volume in a life.

DS: There is volume in each life, and a writer tries (at least sometimes) to turn it up, the better to transcribe the noise. Most people—healthy people—work to turn it down: to find a little quiet in which to live. Maybe that's why it's such a weird job. (Philip Roth: "This profession even fucks up grief.") Anyway.

I'm of a much stronger mind than ever about it now. At least I hope I am. This profession didn't fuck up my grief; it allowed me to feel it, and then at least to begin gesturing past it.

In my friend David Lipsky's excellent book with/about David Foster Wallace, *Although of Course You End Up Becoming Yourself,* Wallace says that a small part of who he is craves fame, but that this part doesn't get to drive. The fact that Celine died is present still in who I am—it would be inhuman if it weren't at least in some way present forever— but it doesn't get to drive my life. I used to wonder what would've happened if Celine had cut in front of a perfect driver, a Mario Andretti. Would that have been enough to save her life? I think not; I think physics dictates that nobody could have avoided her. But I now understand this Andretti vs. Strauss question is useless. She cut in front of me. And I did my best to avoid her. That's all I can control.

I recently heard from a friend of the girl's—someone I never knew. She read *Half a Life* and told me: "Stop beating yourself up. She committed suicide. She talked and even wrote about death constantly in the week before she died." I didn't want to hear that—I don't know if it's true, and it's also not my business. Celine around school seemed happy to me. (Though admittedly I didn't know her well.) I did what I could to avoid hitting her, and that's the only part that concerns me.

All the same, when the book was about to come out, I wanted to write the parents a letter, a warning. Of course, they'd sued me after having said they knew I was blameless— and promising they would always support me. But I never blamed them for anything. (How could I? They'd lost a daughter, and I was walking around.) So I wanted to spare them the pain of being surprised by the book. But the simple act of Googling them and writing the letter was hard—harder than writing the book. It never goes fully away.

CM: Lorca talks about the pulse of the wound that goes through to the opposite side. I suppose that's what you've located. It's a very fine piece of work indeed. More than that, it seems necessary.

DS: This was a wound I didn't acknowledge; I was like Samsa in the beginning of *The Metamorphosis,* unaware I was schlepping around with eight skinny legs and an armor-plated belly. But the messages I've gotten from suffering people—distress signals, really—have strengthened my faith. I was going to say in books, but in everything.

To end on another Bellow (mis)quote, sometimes literary books believe all questions of truth have overwhelmingly formidable answers, uncongenial, hostile to us. It may be, however, that truth is not always so punitive. I learned this. There may be truths on the side of life . . . there may be some truths that are our friends in the universe.

READING GROUP QUESTIONS
AND TOPICS FOR DISCUSSION

1. Strauss includes a number of scenes (of him chatting up girls at the accident site, and of going to the movies later) that portray him in an unfavorable light. Do you think this makes him less likable, or more so? How effective is he in winning your sympathy? Do you think he wants to?

2. It took Strauss half a life to write this book. How do you think it would have differed if he'd tried to write it at the time of the accident? How would it be different if he'd waited another eighteen years?

3. Strauss writes that he thought of college as a "witness protection program"—he went off to school and told basically no one about the accident. Do you think this time was necessary for him to heal, or would he have benefited from talking about the accident to a lot of people right away?

4. As serious as this book is, it does include moments of humor. Strauss pokes gentle fun at "the Shrink"—a psychologist he saw soon after the crash—and at the "Death

& Dying" class he took in college. What purpose do these passages serve in this often somber book?

5. To what degree do you think Strauss's memories were shaped by his age? How reliable is memory after almost two decades?

6. A number of reviewers of this book wrote that, if anything, Strauss was too hard on himself in this memoir. He was found blameless, yet he spent years feeling terrible about the accident. Is that a necessary moral stance, or could he have let himself off the hook a little more?

7. *The Washington Post* wrote that *Half a Life* has a universal appeal, calling it a "penetrating, thought-provoking examination of the human mind." Do you think it raises larger issues beyond the immediate story of the car crash? If so, what are they?

8. Strauss's parents are quite present in the early part of the book, less so as the story progresses. Is this merely a function of the narrator growing older? How would you act differently if it had been your child driving that car on that fateful day?

9. The accident resulted in a lawsuit. Do you think there is some peace of mind to be gained from litigation? Is it a way for us to try to feel better about something awful?

10. Define the relationship between Strauss and his wife, Susannah. How does she differ from the people he'd previously told about the crash?

11. Consider Strauss's choice of career. He writes that, if not for the accident, he may not have become a writer. Does this seem true? Can we be shaped positively by terrible events? If so, how do we ensure that we are?

12. Strauss writes: "There are different brands of ignorance: the static of perplexity, the spun silk of denial." What does this mean?

13. Strauss writes that there was no real epiphanic moment for him, no instant he can point to and say: *That* was when I began to feel better. And yet he seems to have learned a lesson from this event, and by the end of the book he is a changed man. What did he learn?

ABOUT THE AUTHOR

DARIN STRAUSS is the best-selling author of three previous books. The recipient of a Guggenheim in fiction writing and numerous other awards, Strauss has seen his work translated into fourteen languages, and published in more than twenty countries. He is a Clinical Associate Professor of Writing at New York University, and he lives with his wife and children in Brooklyn.

Darin Strauss is available for select readings and lectures. To inquire about a possible appearance, please contact the Random House Speakers Bureau at rhspeakers@randomhouse.com.